THE **STRATEGIC**
WEB DESIGNER

THE STRATEGIC WEB DESIGNER:

How to Confidently Navigate the Web Design Process

Christopher Butler

CINCINNATI, OH
www.howdesign.com

"What strikes me about Chris' book is that he's like a zoom lens. He can see the wide picture and place it in the context of marketing historically, and then zoom right in to how that might impact how any given business would optimize their "pull" strategies to attract the right kind of clients. His writing is clear, buttressed with research and examples, and drags you in to read the whole book at once."

- David C. Baker, Recourses

"No one is thinking more clearly or more intelligently about designing for the web right now than Chris Butler. And now, with his new book The Strategic Web Designer, no one is writing more clearly about it either. As always, Chris employs his trademark conversational approach to present some big ideas about planning, optimizing, and designing your site, and offers valuable tips on what trends to look for on the horizon. All of which will make you not only a better web designer but smarter about the web in general."

- Aaron Kenedi, Editor-in-Chief, Print magazine

"Christopher Butler has created a concise, poetic guide about to how to be strategic about your website work, from planning to prototyping, from measurement to mobile. There are countless resources out there that tell you how to design for the web. But this is one of the few that will help you think critically about how to do it better, and what the future of the web might hold for your practice."

- David Sherwin, author of Creative Workshop: **80 Challenges to Sharpen Your Design Skills and Success by Design: The Essential Business Reference for Designers**

"With this book, Chris introduces a much-needed strategic approach to progressive, bulletproof web design. From the inception of a project to its final release, this book will help you understand the versatile intricacies of the design process, identify common stumbling blocks, and create the solutions your clients need."

- Vitaly Friedman, Editor-in-Chief, **Smashing Magazine**

For more excellent books and resources for designers, visit www.howdesign.com.

16 15 14 13 12   5 4 3 2 1

ISBN-13: 978-1-4403-1502-2

Distributed in Canada by Fraser Direct
100 Armstrong Avenue
Georgetown, Ontario, Canada L7G 5S4
Tel: (905) 877-4411

Distributed in the U.K. and Europe by F&W Media International, LTD
Brunel House, Forde Close, Newton Abbot, TQ12 4PU, UK
Tel: (+44) 1626 323200, Fax: (+44) 1626 323319
Email: enquiries@fwmedia.com

Distributed in Australia by Capricorn Link
P.O. Box 704, Windsor, NSW 2756 Australia
Tel: (02) 4577-3555

Edited by Amy Owen and Scott Francis
Cover desgined by Grace Ring
Interior designed by Ronson Slagle
Production coordinated by Greg Nock

For everyone who loves the web,
even those who are a little afraid of it.

TABLE OF CONTENTS

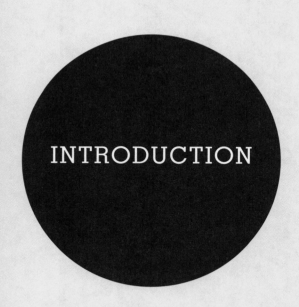

INTRODUCTION

This book won't teach you how to build a website. But it will teach you how to think about the web and, in doing so, prepare you to lead web projects from their inception through the ongoing nurturing process every website requires after launch. That's what web strategy is all about: having a comprehensively informed point of view about the web that enables you to guide a web project intentionally, rather than reactively.

Consider this quote:

> A well-trained man knows how to answer questions; an educated man knows what questions are worth asking.
>
> — *E. Digby Baltzell* [1]

Think about that for a moment. Baltzell's quote gets right at what I hope is the defining characteristic of this book—what separates it from the ocean of valuable, but inherently different, material about the web that is available to you. Web strategy is a scheme for working on the web, elaborate and systematic (as the Princeton definition for strategy[2] specifies), and is born out of a wide and foundational education that includes many things beyond the how-to. But the balance between education and training, or in our case strategy and implementation, is a fine one. No amount of technique will prevent a sudden change in technology from upending your ability to do what you've promised your clients you will do. But a strong foundation in web strategy—the principles by which the web, and work on the web, is conceived—will enable you to keep your bearings as the storm of technological change continues to blow over every "inch" of the web as we know it.

As a design student, I was required to complete an initial year of curriculum called "Foundation Studies" before I was able to choose a specific major of study. During that year, the required courses, which carried deceptively basic titles like Drawing, Two-Dimensional Design, and Three-Dimensional Design, provided a survey of an immense field of knowledge and practice. In my foundation studies, I felt I was exposed to far more knowledge on a variety of things that would not be relevant to my major than was necessary. But once I began my specific course work, I realized how essential that exposure was. In fact, I couldn't possibly have removed one portion of that foundation year; I used every bit of that knowledge throughout the rest of my time in school and continue to do so today, years later. You see, the school laid a foundation for every student that would be as strategically important to them whether they studied painting or landscape architecture. Each department, in turn, laid a similar foundation in its first year and created a structure through which students would gain more and more exposure to specific techniques and practice (as well as individual creative freedom) as the semesters progressed. As many of my classmates would likely say, we learned first how to think about design, then how to do it.

So that's what this book is all about: learning first how to think about the web and web projects so that you can truly take the lead in the way your clients are hoping you will. Where it doesn't cover specific techniques, it will point you to the current best resources that will. But fear not: It will cover a great deal.

In chapter 1, we'll take a big step back and cleanse our palettes with an exploration of what the web is and what it means to do web work. Having done that, we'll then dig deep into planning and look at the entire web development process in detail in chapter 2. Chapter 3 will introduce us to the real people using our websites and some ways we can better get to know them. Chapters 4, 5 and 6 will explore the essential web disciplines: how we organize our websites, optimize their content for searchers and then measure their effectiveness. In chapter 7, we'll pause to explore content at a high level—what it is, why we create it and how we can do better—before looking at some practical considerations for web content marketing. In chapter 8, we'll explore mobile technology and its effect on the web before concluding with a look into the future of the web in chapter 9. Finally, the Notes section contains all kinds of information that I encourage you to explore, from references to expansions on points, as well as resources to assist you in further investigations of just about everything covered in this book.

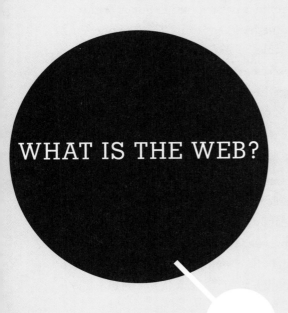

WHAT IS THE WEB?

Everyone knows what the web is, right? I'm actually not so sure.

In a highly unscientific survey[1], I asked around and received a variety of descriptions. Here is a representative sample of them:

> It's a window to the world ... through which you can meet people from anywhere and find virtually any piece of information that exists.

> It's a constantly available and accessible answer to almost any fact-based question you have.

> It's a digital network of content.

These definitions, gathered from people within my network (which certainly leans digital), should theoretically be accurate. But as I read through them, it is evident that something is missing. The first one describes the web as a tool that enables us to find answers to questions. On the other hand, the second describes the web as the answer itself. The third removes the distinction altogether. In light of the first two, perhaps the third suggests that web content can be either a question or an answer, depending upon you.

These three descriptions of the web are indicative of the struggle we have with being able to distinguish between what the web is and what the web enables us to do. While some people tend toward one description more than the other, most depend so heavily upon metaphor that their collective purpose—the meaning they are intended to provide—is lost. It's as if I were to ask for a description of air. I might hear anything from the chemical makeup of our atmosphere to how we'd die without it, but its ubiquity is sure to make a pithy account hard to come by.

So, then, what is the web? Does it have an identity separate from its content, its uses or even the tools we use to access it? Is the web actually something, or is it just an idea?

As a next step, I thought that studying the origin of the web might help to clarify these questions. Here, from his original 1989 proposal[2] for the World Wide Web, is Tim Berners-Lee's description of his intent for the web—what it would be and how it would work:

> The WWW [World Wide Web] project merges the techniques of information retrieval and hypertext to make an easy but powerful global information system.
>
> The project is based on the philosophy that much academic information should be freely available to anyone. It aims to allow information sharing within internationally dispersed teams, and the dissemination of information by support groups. Originally aimed at the High Energy Physics community, it has spread to other areas and attracted much interest in user support, resource discovery and collaborative work areas.
>
> The WWW world consists of documents and links. Indexes are special documents, which, rather than being read, may be searched. The result of such a search is another ("virtual") document containing links to the documents found. A simple protocol ("HTTP") is used to allow a browser program to request a keyword search by a remote information server.
>
> The web contains documents in many formats. Those documents which are hypertext (real or virtual) contain links to other documents, or places within documents. All documents, whether real, virtual or indexes, look similar to the reader and are contained within the same addressing scheme.
>
> To follow a link, a reader clicks with a mouse (or types in a number if he or she has no mouse). To search and index, a reader gives keywords (or other search criteria). These are the only operations necessary to access the entire world of data.

Reading what the creator of the web had to say about his creation certainly helps to sharpen my sense of what the web actually is: a collection of connected digital files made freely accessible by the internet and navigable by standard hardware. And yet, Berners-Lee's proposal still does not provide an entirely complete description of the web. It certainly doesn't sound much like the web I know. After all, it was written over twenty years ago. Stopping there would make as much sense as assuming the birth account of an infant is still the most accurate description of the adult she has grown to become. That is, unless the web is the same today as it was in 1989. Of course, it isn't. Not even close.

Coincidentally, one of my younger brothers was also born in 1989. Today, with clear memories of changing his diapers, teaching him simple new things and hearing him learn his first words, I marvel at the man he has become. He is now the almost inconceivably complex result of his genes, the environment in which he was raised, the many people he has known and every piece of information he has ever encountered—not to mention a million other things my simplistic description leaves out. Though not a person, the web is, in some ways, similarly personalized; its present makeup is also the result of a multitude of complexities and personalities. Author E.B. White, in a letter written to inspire the children of Troy, Michigan, to use their new public library, described books as people—"people who have managed to stay alive by hiding between the covers of a book."[3] Indeed, is the web not similarly atemporal, absorbing and storing bits of us one day and changing us the next—not to mention similarly divergent, serving as one's hideaway and another's stage? But I digress ...

The point is that at the time of this writing, my brother is still an undergraduate student—his career undetermined, his future, largely unknown. He is still just beginning his life. The web is, no doubt, on a winding road to maturity as well. With the same two decades behind it, the web enters a third—just as my brother does—as a very young adult, still assembling an identity largely under the influence of myriad external forces.

Pushing the child-raising metaphor just a bit further, the web, unlike any other child in human history, has been mostly raised in community, given to us by its "father" to shape and nurture together. This makes us just as responsible for the web as is its creator. For better or worse, we bear the full weight of the web's identity, which also means that the web will be no better, nor worse, than we are. Indeed, looking at the web reveals much of the human experience. Within it can be found the beauty of love, compassion, charity, gratitude, the wonder of creation, inspiration, joy and truth, as well as the darkness of hatred, spite, envy, greed, lust, shame, jadedness, sorrow, grief and lies. No effort to purge it of its dark side will be any more possible than doing so within ourselves, nor will the dark side ever fully eclipse the light. They may, at times, be out of balance, but one will never subsume the other. The web, I believe, will always reflect back upon us our own complex and often contradictory character.

The diverse texture of the web can be felt in the many forms of expression it contains. Just as intimacy with anyone will reveal the capacity for a great many behaviors—both the rash and the considered—the web, as a library of human experience, should not surprise you with what it contains. Books alongside the detritus of archived instant communications, essays and comment threads, laws and local crime reports, scientific studies and pseudoscience, gossip and fact, prayers and threats, manifestos, pleas ... and that's just the text. The images, video and audio are just as varied and extensive. Frank Rose put it well when he described the web as "a chameleon." In *The Art of Immersion*, he elaborates[4]:

[The web is] the first medium that can act like all media—it can be text, or audio, or video, or all of the above ... It is inherently participatory—not just interactive, in the sense that it responds to your commands, but an instigator constantly encouraging you to comment, to contribute, to join in. And it is immersive—meaning you can use it to drill down as deeply as you like about anything you care to.

On the whole, the web represents our willingness to explore who we are. Our curiosity and imagination have left behind a frank display of a culture far beyond that which we are capable of individually experiencing.

If anyone asks me what the web is, I will answer with what I acknowledge is a definition that perhaps favors the grandeur of experience over the means by which that experience is possible—in other words, more like the first two examples I shared at the beginning of this chapter than the third. But I do so intentionally, as my feeling is that the technology powering the web is far less important (and certainly far less interesting) than the role the web has in representing humanity. In only two decades, in part due to how quickly it has done so, the web has become the largest and most important cultural artifact in human history.

And yet, to bring things back down to Earth, it is still a work in progress.

Long ago, in 2007—and believe me, five years is a long time on the web—I read a column by Harry McCracken, the editor-in-chief of *PC World*, that I have not been able to forget since[5]. In marveling at the pace of technological change, and its increasing scope of reach across the world, he wrote:

More than any communications medium before it, the web is a permanent work in progress that's always new.

I've probably repeated that line hundreds of times since then—to colleagues and clients alike—in order to impress upon them this truth that we will never be finished. I've made it my mantra. And really, this is the central, most profound distinction between the web and almost any other medium in existence, especially from a designer's perspective. While a printed piece moves in one direction, from inception through design and production to the point at which I can hold it in my hands and keep it, web content moves forward and backward in an endlessly undulating pattern, from idea to implementation, there and back again.

Work that is never finished, that changes everything. Our design thinking, the processes we follow, the way we estimate costs and plan schedules, the promises we make, the way we measure success—every facet of the practice of design looks very different when considered in light of the web. But the fundamentals of design, those truths by which we judge design to be good or bad, do not change. This means that designers, though they may naturally specialize in one form of practice over another, need not feel permanently unqualified for interactive work simply because their primary experience has been in print. In fact, if the web is a permanent work in progress, as I agree with McCracken it is, then no one can be permanently unqualified to contribute to that progress. So, I also like to think of our contributions—our web work—in the same way.

Imagine being a child again, sitting on the living room floor, surrounded by blocks. In your mind is a grand vision for a tower unlike any other known to the world, one that only imagination could realize and wooden blocks can only approximate (though thankfully, you don't yet know this). You start piling blocks, without any plan other than the picture in your mind and the desire to create. In truth, you're not exactly building this tower, you're discovering it, shaping it intuitively as you respond to the rubble around you. And there's no deadline. You've got all the time in the world ... That is, until Mom calls you for dinner.

If you're like me, the artist in you still entertains romantic David Macaulay-esque construction fantasies like this one at the outset of most projects you undertake. You begin them with the wonder of child only to be quickly thrust into the practical realities of adult work plans, personnel, budgets, schedules, resources, deadlines and management. Within minutes of getting started, wonder is often replaced with worry. The dreamer in me might find this a bit sad, but I've learned two important things that bring me solace:

1. Web projects are successful when practicality and creativity meet in appropriate measure.

2. If my whimsy has to take a step back for the sake of the project (which it often does), I'll always have my living room floor ...

Surely you have already learned this lesson, so I don't need to go on about it much more than to leave it at this: While the web, as I've examined it so far, can be a philosopher's playground, web projects involve far less play and much more ground. They are the result of both an apprehension of the web's meaning and the covering of the ground of implementation—a complex meeting of design and technology shaped by many people who must work to maintain a common vision. It's this "complex meeting" idea that could probably use some further elaboration. To do just a piece of that, let me return to the construction metaphor, but with a dose of reality.

If you've ever been involved in building a house, you already have some insight into how building a website really works. Before any wood is cut, thousands of decisions are made, from finding land to choosing the knobs on the kitchen cabinets. In between is a wide spectrum of issues that concern many players: the architects, developers, construction workers, interior designers, landscapers and, of course, the customer. With the cost of the design and construction of a house, you'd expect the project to require the focus, diligence and consistency of everyone involved, which unfortunately leaves little room for play. (In fact, experimentation is guaranteed to take most clients from wonder to worry lickety-split.) I think you see where I'm going here.

Web projects are just like this.

Because web technology makes so much room for iteration (unlike building houses), they must be managed even more carefully. A print project makes a significant technological transition from design to production—from the screen to the print shop—which is costly enough to keep it from happening in reverse. But the time-bending, causality-looping, iterative nature of the web allows web projects, on the other hand, to move forward and backward across a narrower technological gap that often makes it too easy to do ad nauseam until, *whoops!*, you're way over budget with no real way to reverse the trend. Not good. To be avoided.

As I ruminate on one of the differences between print and web projects, I realize that I run the risk of making working on the web out to be drudgery. I don't want to do that; I assure you, working on the web is fun. For designers, the need for discipline and moderation is nothing new and is certainly neither a killjoy nor the really interesting thing about working on the web. The really interesting part is in the work—what you're reading this book to learn more about, I assume. Think about the building analogies I've used. Buildings and homes are obviously the results of long, costly and complex processes. But a striking difference is that while buildings can be constructed with almost no direct input from the consumer—few homeowners have much more than a spectator's role while construction is under way—a good website cannot be built without significant involvement from the client throughout every stage of the project. It is this difference that requires anyone anticipating a web project to be well versed in the process: designers, so they know how to guide their client, and clients, so they know what to expect and how to answer the many, many questions they'll be asked along the way. That means there is much to plan for and even more to learn.

But before we move into thinking about planning, I want to provide you with one more connection back to matters of purpose. This has to do with the common vision I mentioned earlier, the one to which we must cling as an imperative throughout a project, not just until the vicissitudes of life derail it.

Think back, for a moment, to the last time you unwrapped a fast-food burger (vegetarians, forgive me). Now compare that image—the burger you received—with the way the restaurant portrayed that burger in its advertising and its menu. Are they two different burgers? Probably. Unfortunately[6]. One is The Burger—a burger on steroids: its bun, a perfect golden brown, smooth edges, evenly coated with sesame seeds as if they rained from the sky; its crisp lettuce and tomato, the most saturated green and red you've ever seen; its beef patty, evenly grilled as if by a master chef; the entire thing, sunlit and glistening with the moist anticipation of being eaten. The other, your burger, is the undead—the way you might expect a quasi food to look—resurrected from cryonic preservation and kept on life support by heat lamps before it is consumed under the sickly pale of institutional fluorescent light. The Burger is a promise; your burger is that promise broken.

Maybe the comedown from The Burger to your burger doesn't surprise you. On the contrary, you have probably come to expect disappointment from products produced en masse. Unfortunately, you are not alone. Our low-level, day-to-day state of jadedness induced by the ubiquity of insincere marketing—the kind that blinds us to what otherwise would look like satire, deflating the hilarity (and then, outrage) that should ensue from broken commercial promises—makes experiencing surprise and delight in the world that much more rare. I don't think it's put too strongly to say that cynicism is the gravity that you are working against in every project you undertake. The antidote is authenticity. It is proven when a product or service actually delivers on its promises, and it is possible. After all, is it not extraordinary that some brands profit by cooperating with our cynicism? And I do mean cooperate: Our willingness to eat disappointing burgers is complicity; by consuming, we enable the spread of disappointment.

With the bitter taste of disappointment still on your tongue, I want you to now consider your web project—the one you're anticipating or even the one already in process. Are there promises within your vision that you suspect you may break? Holding firm to a clear sense of motive will naturally moderate your inclination to overpromise, whether that is to yourself, your superiors or your client. The other tool you'll have at your disposal—reality—should even more strongly manage your expectations and guide your planning. I'll cover this (in great detail) in the next chapter.

Knowing why you're building a website seems simple enough, doesn't it? But you'd be amazed to know just how often web projects reach significant milestones only to fail to launch because their purpose wasn't as clear as everyone assumed. Depending upon your level of involvement in the project—whether you're working on your own website or one for a client—you have the opportunity and responsibility to ask this question again and again. Directed at one's self, it will regularly exercise a healthy scrutiny and provide balance to your subjectivity. Inviting your client into a culture of questioning sets a powerful precedent early in your relationship, affirming your strategic role and provoking thoughtful engagement with them, rather than order taking at the beginning and finger pointing later. So, a mantra for you: Purpose at inception, and thereafter.

PLANNING WEB
PROJECTS

I don't have to know much about your web project to guess that its timeline is all wrong. In my experience, web projects always take longer than they are expected to—not just because of avoidable delays (there will be some), but because they simply need more time than they are given. So, first things first: You might as well slow down. You're going to need some time at the outset to think this thing through, identify the right goals, plan a process that will facilitate them and allow time to do the work itself. Oh, and let's not forget time for testing before launch. Lots and lots of testing.

Most web planning is reactive, prompted by an upcoming date by which the new website should be launched, otherwise ... well, that's a good question, actually. Otherwise, what? The anxiety brought about by a looming date—that trade show coming up, for instance—can set in motion an extraordinary push to get the house in order. But anxiety is, without question, an unhealthy catalyst for a complex web project and a poison for one already underway. Often the rationale is that an anticipated event will bring throngs of discerning and expectant visitors to your door and the current website is just not fit to be seen. And it may very well not be. Of course, little thought is given at this point to the alternative—that a rushed replacement might be far more unfit to receive guests than the current site.

It is often at this point—after the decision to rebuild is made and anxiety well set in—that those tasked with the new web project are brought into the discussion. The conversation tends to go something like this:

Boss: "We need a new website, and it needs to be live by January 1."

You: "..."

It's actually not much of a discussion, is it? Even more troubling is that these New Year's resolution pronouncements tend to be made far too late to have any hope of satisfying anyone's expectations. I've heard plenty of them, though: They begin as November news, turn into December desperation and settle at January just-get-it-done—a painful phase that tends to last for many more months, making failure the status quo. By then, though the big event that got the ball rolling in the first place may have long passed, the stress remains. No matter what the new deadline becomes, it's not likely to change the outcome: the launch of a mediocre (at best) website. Haste makes waste.

But back to November. As you made your way back to your desk after that meeting, you probably wondered when planning for that event (let's call it a trade show—it's always a trade show) had really begun. Probably long before November, right? Things like trade shows take much longer than two months to plan; not only do many of the details have to be worked out far in advance—things like facilities and vendors—but so do the invitations. So why did the decision to launch a new website come so much later?

Deadlines, Productivity and Other Opportunities for Denial

Suppose you have been invited to a dinner party. You'd like to bring a dessert, so you look up a cake recipe and learn that preparation will take around two hours. If dinner is at seven o'clock, you should plan to start sometime around five, right? Not quite. Realistically you're probably going to need more than just two hours before the dinner starts for preparation— time the recipe is probably not taking into account in its estimate. The entire process, which includes the time to gather the ingredients, to mix the batter, to bake, to let the cake cool, to wash the pans and utensils, and finally, to frost the cake, is surely longer than that. And that assumes you don't get interrupted. If you don't give yourself enough time to do this right, you're going to end up with a mess in a bowl, which means you're either bringing nothing or buying a cake. I once worked at a bakery, and last-minute cake order situations were common, but they were also a lot like the last-minute website planning I witness today: While you might try to get something at the last minute, it will either be impossible (good bakeries don't tend to sell old cakes), expensive or disappointing.

Underestimating time is endemic in web work, so squeezed production schedules are much more common than they should be. But this planning problem creates a more toxic perception problem. Given the time made available to do the work—often underestimated, mind you—we assume our productivity will be greater than average. We don't soberly assess our limitations. You think you don't do this, but trust me, you do. We all do. Just imagine the last time you injured yourself or were ill (I'm remembering tearing my rotator cuff a couple of years ago). We tend to do two perplexing things in these situations: The first is that we ignore the affliction for far too long, underestimating its severity and assuming it will just go away in a few days. That's the planning problem. Meanwhile, we don't rest and end up doing more damage until we can no longer ignore the injury. When we finally do get medical attention, we're told that recovery could take weeks and that we're going to have to change our behavior to make it happen. After a few days, we start to feel a bit better and proudly consider ourselves exceptions to the rule. We're stronger than average, right? Wrong. When we're not patient and don't trust the doctor's advice, we end up right back in her office, worse than before. The perception problem becomes a reality problem.

The strange thing is that far fewer people probably rush baking a cake than their own recoveries. Yet rushing the cake isn't likely to cost much more than the ingredients and the cake you buy to replace your rushed mess-in-a-bowl. Rushing a rotator cuff recovery, on the other hand, is potentially far more costly. I certainly don't know of any store that could sell me a quick replacement. Why do we do this? It all comes down to the way we manage expectations. In these instances, our many expectations are often led by impatience—the expectation of *now*. But when *now* leads the charge, all the other things that matter, like quality, efficiency, cost and the like, are crippled. In fact, none of our expectations can be met if we are not willing to properly facilitate them, and especially not if they're misinformed in the first place.

In an ideal world, planning for your web project would have begun as soon as the date of the trade show was known, which, let's be honest, was long before November.

This is true of any project, really. Take this book, for example. I began discussions with the publisher to write it in November 2010. It took another two months or so before the project was approved, at which point

I received a contract and the green light to get started. At the outset, I had assumed I could get all the writing done in six months and would be able to deliver my manuscript in June. The publisher, on the other hand, had other, better-informed ideas about how long it would take; they asked that I deliver the first half of the manuscript in September. The rushed-recovery mentality kicked right in, and I thought, "Well, I'm faster than average. This will be a piece of cake." Working with writers on book projects is what publishers do every day; I should have taken their assessment of the time I'd need more seriously rather than assuming that I, a first-time book author, had any idea what was realistic. My overconfidence and unrealistic opinion toward the time writing this book would require was exactly the kind of posture I'd seen taken time and again by clients planning their web projects.

I am not saying that deadlines should not motivate a project. On the contrary, deadlines are absolutely necessary! It was the September deadline that I had in my mind every single day since January that motivated me to continually face an empty screen and write. The difference is that it was a realistic deadline—barring any procrastination on my part, of course. A January deadline for a web project set in November, on the other hand, is not realistic. Remember, most web project schedules aren't blown because of procrastination or avoidable delays. Most were never solvent in the first place.

I may have severely belabored this point, but it's been my experience that one cannot overemphasize the need for a healthy dose of realism—informed by the right process—in scheduling web work. Now, with our hubris firmly in check, we can examine what that process should be and what kind of time it may demand.

The Ideal Web Development Process

There are many factors that will determine the process of designing and building a website. In particular, the scope of the project itself—the general size of the site, the level of complexity and other functional requirements—should be the primary driver of the amount of time, resources and personnel that are devoted to completing it. But on a more general level, there are some categoric factors to consider—those that have more to do with the business context in which the project exists, whether for the advertising agency, interactive firm or the end client themselves. These include things related to the positioning of the agency or interactive firm—what kind of work they do and for whom—as well as the technologies they are prepared to utilize. As you may imagine, these factors are widespread and diverse, which means they could result in very different approaches. The process that I will review here is certainly malleable and scalable around these factors. The key concepts to glean here are more about identifying the proper sequence for a web project's phases, as well as general ratios of time from one phase to another.

The remainder of this chapter will provide an overview of the entire web development process. While complete in and of itself, it is by no means exhaustive, and many of the concepts involved will be explored in greater detail in later chapters. Additionally, there are some concepts—especially those involved with technique such as design, development and quality assurance—that receive a light treatment here and throughout the book. My reasoning here is in three parts: (1) As I emphasized in the introduction, this book is about web strategy, focused more on the *why* than the *how*. (2) Web design and programming disciplines are the core skills that many readers of this book already bring to the table. (3) There are many excellent titles already available by authors with much greater expertise on those subjects than I could possibly offer. Indeed, I will certainly recommend many of them along the way. So, with that said, let's begin.

	CONTENT CREATION	CONTENT ENTRY		
PROTOTYPING	PROGRAMMING	DESIGN APPLICATION	Q.A.	LAUNCH
	DESIGN			

An initial consulting phase may not be necessary for every project, but there are plenty of situations in which it would be wise to set aside focused time—anywhere from one week to a month, depending upon the overall size of the project—to work through a strategic approach to the website. In general, this is an ideal time to identify and discuss the purpose behind the project, the intended audience (something I'll cover specifically in chapter 3) and the goals of the website. You want to assemble a big-picture view of the scope of the project based upon this information. While many of these questions were probably asked during the period in which the project was priced and acquired (assuming this is not an in-house project), returning to elaborate and gain more detail about their answers before proceeding further in is important. To be clear, this consulting phase involves no production at all. It exists simply to ensure that everyone involved is clear on the project's strategy and intended objectives. The bigger the team, the bigger the need for it.

For projects involving entrepreneurial ventures or businesses transitioning to operating online for the first time, front-loading the process with time to go over, in detail, the role the website will have within the overall business is critical. Without that time, assumptions are guaranteed to be made (by everyone) during subsequent phases that will orient the project in one direction—perhaps in terms of design or functionality—that could be extremely costly to reverse later.

Remember the question I posed earlier in the chapter addressing the why of your project? Realistically, you or your client may need help answering that question. In general, most sites are created to enable sales—either for businesses selling to other businesses (B2B) or for businesses selling to consumers (B2C). But how the website factors into the sales process will be very different in either scenario. These two general categories provide a natural starting point from which you can guide your team diagnostically toward properly identifying the purpose and strategy of the website.

B2B Websites

B2B (business to business) websites can be divided into two basic categories: those that offer services and those that offer products. For businesses that offer services, the immediate goals of their website should be to capture the attention of prospects that don't yet know about them, speak directly to their need by clearly identifying pain points and solutions, and compel them to action. From there, the off-line sales process can kick in, but with a far more qualified lead. In other words, B2B service websites are primarily informational resources and lead-generation tools. B2B product websites, on the other hand (e.g., those for software or hardware products), will probably need to include more advanced functionality sets comprising product demos, sales support, customer support forums and e-commerce, in addition to the informational resources and marketing content that services provide to grow and sustain their business.

B2C Websites

B2C (business to consumer) websites can also be divided into two categories: those that need to build new brand awareness and those that need to maintain and grow existing brand awareness. It seems like a subtle distinction, but much of the tactical off-site work that will rely upon close integration with the website—like online and off-line advertising, direct mail and e-mail, and social media marketing campaigns—will look very different depending upon which stage the business is in. Like a B2B product website, however, more advanced functionality will probably be nonnegotiable for the scope of a B2C website project. Specifically e-commerce functionality—enabling users to browse an online store and make purchases—will be important, if not the central purpose of the website itself.

This is just one diagnostic starting place. It probably seems too simple, but that is the point: The "obvious" stuff is usually forgotten or set aside in preference for details that are not relevant until the big-picture goals are established and agreed upon by the entire team. What isn't obvious is how easy it is to lose sight of those goals as time passes. Make the starting place your working mantra so that you never find yourself designing something that has nothing to do with where you began (e.g., "… and we want a weather feed on the home page next to the featured product slide show." Sound familiar?). Imagine if some restaurants stuck to their basic goals? Remember, those that do not will serve up broken promises.

There are, of course, plenty of other kinds of websites than just the basic categories I mentioned. But the basic distinction should provide a good planning rubric for most of the projects that come your way. Whatever the case may be, you must set specific goals for your website early and stick by them throughout the rest of the process.

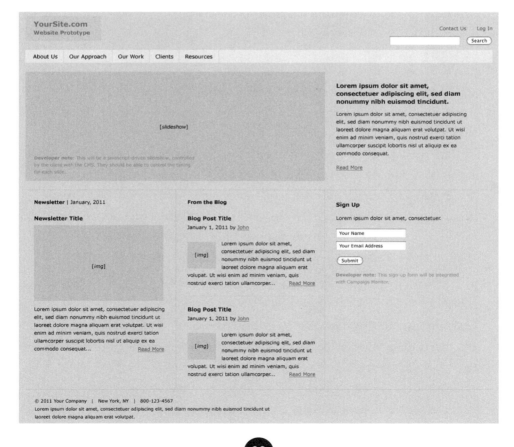

Prototyping

I have devoted the entirety of chapter 5 to information architecture—much of which will explain why website prototypes are most effective in an interactive form—so rather than include material here that would make much of that chapter redundant, I'd like to briefly explain what I mean by prototyping and share some observations on how to plan for the prototyping process.

Rather than a static representation of a website's structure and contents, which is essentially what site maps and wireframes are, a website prototype is a clickable, aesthetically neutral version of a website created in an iterative and collaborative process—by a team comprised of those representing planning, design, and development, as well as the end client—before any visual design or programming has begun. Because visual design considerations are so powerful and can shape decisions that should be made independent of their influence, a prototype should not include any visual distinctions other than those that might be necessary to indicate the hierarchy and priority of information on a page. For this reason, my firm has intentionally referred to them as "grayscreen" prototypes to emphasize the absence of aesthetic factors in the prototyping process. While certainly not to diminish the importance of design, prototypes should be focused on the structure of a website, its informational content and its intended functionality. These three areas of focus are more thoroughly explained in chapter 5.

In the sample project schedule at the beginning of this section, the prototyping phase has been given a month of time. While that may seem like plenty of time, it's probably not enough. This particular schedule itself comes from a sample of my firm's project data from 2010 and is the default we use to schedule most new projects. But of the twenty-two unique website projects we worked on in 2010, all of them took more than one month to produce a complete prototype approved by everyone involved. In fact, the average prototyping time span among these projects was 1.75 months. While many were closer to the one month planned, several outliers took four months or more to resolve. Because there are multiple points of approval in a process like this, it is difficult to be exact in scheduling milestones. It is better to plan a process in which the various phases can adjust and cascade based upon when key milestones occur.

It is not likely that prototyping will require full-time attention during these spans of time. At that rate, a prototype scheduled over a one-month time period could be expected to require 160 hours from a four-person team. But because most design and interactive firms are managing multiple projects simultaneously, a schedule like this one assumes part-time attention from those involved. In fact, from my 2010 project data set, the average amount of prototyping hours logged by our employees—including both the client meetings and the implementation—was 51 hours. Meanwhile, most of our development teams were working on one to two other website projects simultaneously.

Spreading these hours over a month of time, rather than cramming them into one week, actually contributes to the efficiency of the process and solvency of the decision making. Planning, in whatever form it takes, needs space to let strategic ideas settle in our minds. Working around the clock on a prototype is more likely to rush that process and produce a less considered and cogent result. Our teams operate on a schedule of two roughly hour-long prototype meetings per week with our clients, which provides more than enough time to get into detail, as well as enough space in between to gather information on both sides and implement new decisions into the prototype itself. The fact that the average time span for prototyping actually exceeded the month originally scheduled also indicates that biweekly planning sessions, while possible for some of our busy clients, was a slightly faster pace than most could handle.

Design Creation

Most readers of this book are probably very well versed in design. Because I've written it with designers in mind, I don't intend to delve very far into core design matters, though I would like to review the process by which design for the web is created. Naturally, I think this is best explained by turning to music.

Designing for the web is more like jazz than a symphony. When you design for print, you can control just about every detail, finely crafting your vision and then conducting the production each step along the way. Similarly, classical composers write every note in advance, even including instructions for how the notes are to be played. The web, on the other hand, offers far less opportunity for control. When you design for the web, you start with a creative vision and then set up rules that everyone else involved in creating content from that point forward can follow. But you only have as much control as your initial plan allows you to have; once the website is live, it becomes shaped by its content. The design you initially created serves more as a brand standard for the website, just like the initial key and tempo off of which jazz musicians riff.

Additionally, design for the web involves much more than simply styling what has been prototyped with images, colors and fonts. It is also more than selecting a fashionable template that fits with current visual web trends. Design is a process that continues to build upon decisions made in the prototype, focusing on how the visual presentation reinforces the purpose of the website while also clearly communicating the character of the brand. Beginning with a discovery stage that combines an understanding of the intended audience identified in the planning phase with other critical information—like existing brand standards and marketing campaigns, positioning documentation, and other feedback gathered from clients or customers—the design phase begins with the creation of mood boards[1] and then, once the look and feel presented by them is approved, the template-specific layouts.

Creating mood boards for the web is like visual prototyping. Like traditional mood boards, web mood boards compile inspirational elements, color palette, typography, and texture in a context that emulates the screen but is not page-template specific. At this stage in the design process, it is more important to make bigger-picture design decisions than to consider how specific pages of the website will look, down to the pixel. In other words, mood boards establish a site's look and feel in the same way that a brand-standards document specifies how a brand is represented in various contexts. Rather than including the actual layout of a products list page, it will specify which type styles, sizes and edge treatment of images and other details, such as buttons and spacing, are used in lists throughout the site. Once the mood boards are approved, the design of site page templates is a much more efficient process since the more personal issues that tend to stall design decision making have already been made.

Because the mood board is not concerned with specific page template layouts, it can be developed concurrently with the prototype. This keeps design-related discussions from interfering with the prototyping process, but it also engages design thinking early in the process. Being able to see the look and feel take shape this early is often encouraging and motivating—a good thing since maintaining a steady pace is critical to keeping the design phase on schedule and budget.

Like any other design process, foundational decisions support and enable other, more detail-oriented decisions. Since the mood board has already worked out the valuable thinking that goes into the design, the subsequent

| LAYOUT OF PAGE ELEMENTS | PROPORTIONS, SPACING, TYPE STYLES, ICONS, ETC. | SPECIFIC IMAGE CHOICES |

articulation of that design can be a much more streamlined process. Beginning with the basic arrangement of elements within the layout, decisions in this phase should follow a narrowing funnel, gradually focusing and ending with less consequential issues, like what particular stock image is used in a promotional area far down the page.

Violating this funnel can be quite costly. If the entire color palette is called into question several weeks into the design of page layouts, or even after the mood board has been approved, the entire team would have to consider the cost (in time and resources) of going back to the start of the process. Something so foundational will naturally have a broad, sweeping impact upon other design decisions that, in and of themselves, are less significant.

Before the layout design process is complete, it's important to do one last review to make sure there are no remaining inconsistencies with the prototype, that the correct fonts are provided and licensed and that any stock imagery used has been accounted for and purchased. Once the design is approved, the designer can pass it (ideally, in layered and labeled Adobe Photoshop documents) on to the developer to apply to the site, which, as the timeline indicates, should already be in progress.

Programming

Once the prototype has been approved, the programming team should have all they need to begin building a functional website. Their work, assuming a fully functional, modern marketing website, should consist of constructing a database integrated with a content management system (CMS), creating the site's structure and unique page templates first and then applying the final visual design to the site. Just as prototyping and design are isolated as distinct processes, so should the programming of the website be separate from the application of the visual design. This allows the team to focus first on the logic of how a site operates before worrying about how it will look.

As a new website is being built, it should look somewhat similar to the prototype. (At my firm, we call unskinned websites "whitescreens" to highlight the distinction between them and their prototypes.) But while it may look like the prototype—in that no visual design has been applied yet—the whitescreen is very different. It actually works! The developer defines every type of content (i.e., products, articles, blogs, whitepapers, among others) as unique records in the website's database. Each content type's record will be defined by multiple variables, such as its title, abstract,

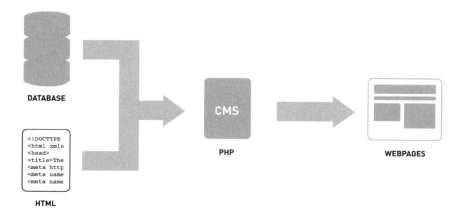

DATABASE

```
<!DOCTYPE
<html xmln
<head>
<title>The
<meta http
<meta name
<meta name
```

HTML

CMS

PHP

WEBPAGES

main content, images, etc. Then, the developer configures the main templates to retrieve that content as needed.

Unlike a static HTML web page, a CMS-driven website will process the raw data that sits in a website's database and match it with the correct HTML for the page template it belongs on, producing the web page as we see it through a browser. As the diagram below indicates, the language the

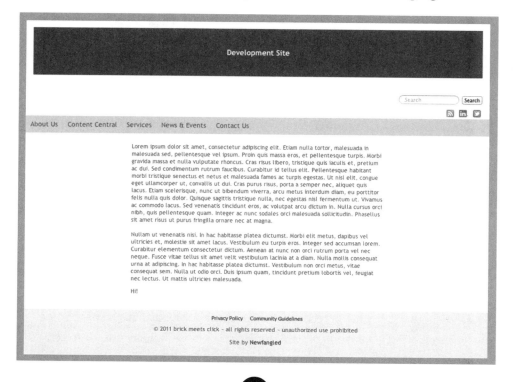

developer uses (PHP, for example) exists within the CMS, executing scripts that are written to produce specific results.[2]

The sample whitescreen shown here is a good example of how retrieval works. At the top of the page, a "test slide" is displaying. In this site's database, a "slide" is particular type of content that, in addition to having a main image, has a title, a description and links to another page on the site. However, the home page has been designed to display an interactive slide show that allows the user to browse through all the slides. This is achieved by the CMS, which runs a script to retrieve each "slide" record in the database and place it in the page. Now, the user can use the arrow buttons to view multiple slides without having to refresh the page.

By the way, when I said that the whitescreen actually works, I meant that quite literally. Because the site is so thoroughly integrated with its CMS, those who will maintain the site later can actually begin using the site before the visual design is applied. Having access to the site once the whitescreen is complete is a great way to maximize the amount of time available for content entry—something that can derail a project's time line very easily. Of the sample data I mentioned earlier, almost every project saw a greater delay due to content entry than at any other point in the process. I'll share some more thoughts about content entry later in this chapter.

Design Application

A website's design is a critical component of its ability to properly communicate. It sets the tone and gives voice to a brand speaking to a potentially wide audience across the web. Because the structure and logic of the site has already been worked out during the whitescreen stage, the developer can now focus solely on the visual detail and interactive effects that enable the website's voice during design application.

The developer refers to the Photoshop document (PSD) created by the designer, which contains every image, color and typeface used in the design. The designer also provides a stylesheet that lists the specific colors, sizes and weights of various text styles that will be used repeatedly throughout the site (i.e., headlines, sub-headlines, link styles, and others). With all this information, the developer can create cascading style sheets (CSS) that the site templates are matched with in order to display according to the design. With one master CSS and others related to unique templates, any future changes to the style of the site need only be made in one place.[3]

Quality Assurance and Integration

Quality Assurance (QA), is defined well by the online Project Management glossary[4]:

> A planned and systematic pattern of all actions necessary to provide adequate confidence that the item or product conforms to established technical requirements.

In other words, QA is a standardized method that ensures that everything works as it was intended to work and looks as it was intended to look. QA for the web should include an initial site-specific test plan, a round of browser testing and a generous integration phase during content entry, enabling functionality to be evaluated in the context of use.[5]

Every website built around a CMS will have a significant amount of common functionality that will require testing. This kind of general evaluation might include anything from testing the CMS login process to exporting website form data, but it is not primarily concerned with how things appear visually. Of course, if something is radically out of place visually, it should be noted. However long the testing list, this first step should be focused on identifying any flaws in the standard operation of the site and its CMS and can probably be performed once the whitescreen is complete and before design application has occurred.

The second step is to evaluate functionality specific to the website. Again, this stage is less concerned with how things appear visually than with how things work. For example, an e-commerce website's store should be thoroughly tested with every relevant combination of products, accessories and discount codes to make sure that even the most minor variable isn't overlooked. A site with a large content database that relies heavily upon an advanced search tool should be tested by running a large number of various search queries. A site with complex form options should have many test form submissions sent covering all options and combinations of options, and so on. While the test plan should be drawn up by the team—naturally, those most familiar with how the site is intended to function—the person performing the test plan should be someone familiar with the technology, process and purpose of QA, but new to the particular project being tested. Even if you don't have a dedicated person filling this role, you should endeavor to have fresh eyes on the site for this stage of QA.

Realistically there is going to be some overlap between the test plan and browser testing. Common site functions, like form submissions, for example, can have unpredictable issues in different browsers. But once the site functionality has been thoroughly vetted, the site needs to be tested, page by page, in every browser you opt to officially support. Browser testing can be done in a variety of ways, including running multiple physical machines, running virtual machines locally, running a centralized virtual machine server or using a third-party testing service.[6]

By the way, despite being nine years old and well out of compliance with today's web standards, Internet Explorer 6 is still being used by a considerable portion of the population. While some testing tools make it easy to check out how a website looks in outdated browsers, they don't change the fact that it often requires a lot of extra effort to make a modern site look and function correctly in them. At this point, it doesn't make much sense to do more than ensure that websites degrade well to IE 6; guaranteeing perfect performance in it is a losing battle.[7]

Once the test plan is complete, the site is probably ready for content entry. Remember, this often happens before the design has been applied, so it's important that anyone involved in content entry is prepared to see and use a work in progress. Though it's not officially considered a QA method,

I believe that content entry, or integration, is one of the most effective and important QA efforts for any project.

On that note, a few years back, Glen Whitman posted a web page titled "The Two Things"[8] based upon the premise that "for every subject, there are really only two things you really need to know." When I first encountered this idea, I immediately thought, "What are the two things about the web?" Then they just popped in to my head and I haven't changed them since; both correspond nicely to the fundamentals of QA:

1. It is a work in progress.

2. There will be bugs.

Typically integration—the word I prefer over "content entry"—is the point in a project when the entire team is able to fully experience the site for the first time. While they have worked together on the various phases I've reviewed so far, the process of using the CMS to create and enter content is when all the "dots" are typically connected and made real, and it's often the first point at which expectations are clarified. With that in mind, here's some straight talk: No matter how thorough the prototype is, sometimes there are concepts or needs that cannot be communicated until you are immersed in an actual working and producing environment. This is similar to what I call the "blank-slate shopper" phenomenon. Have you ever seen a review of a book and thought that you'd like to purchase it, only to find that the next time you are actually in a bookstore you have no idea what you want or where to start? This is because we tend towards reactive, rather than proactive, thinking. We hear about a book and react to it with, "Yes, I'd like to read that," yet when we get to the store and are surrounded by thousands of books, we react to them all by drawing a blank. In web development, things are reversed a bit. Prototyping can be like the store, offering lots of attractive options unrefined by the future reality of how a site will be used. "Yes, I'd like my site to do that!" But integration will always catch the flaws in a site, be they many or few, because users will more quickly react to what they can't do than what they expected to be able to. "Sure, the slide show is nice, but I need to change the address in the footer!"

Finally, QA does not ensure that a project will be 100 percent bug free. While some bugs are due to sloppiness or haste and can be quickly identified by QA, others are the result of unforeseen functionality conflicts that may not become evident until a site has been used for a while—despite the best intentions and foresight of the team. As with any development project, bugs like these should be expected and encountered with patience. (Need I remind you of how buggy some expensive operating systems are when they launch?) While the various steps of QA are intended to mitigate the frequency of any bugs occurring, you should not be surprised when they show up.

Now, back to the content side of integration.

Have you ever arrived to help a friend move only to find that they're still packing boxes? This happens all the time; usually the final "push" involves cramming random loose items in the seats of your car—you know, that last picture from the living room, the blender, a bunch of hangers and a basketball ...

The thing is, no matter how well you plan for moving day, it's very difficult to accurately visualize reorganizing the stuff that fills your home into small cardboard boxes. It's like the ultimate game of Tetris—when the rows start dropping faster, you leave all kinds of gaps in between blocks while trying to keep up. Evidently, what's true about moving physical things is also true about moving information: There is probably more to move than you thought—and less time to move it.

I've seen all kinds of stressful things happen during the content entry phase of a project. Sometimes the content hasn't even been created yet, so the time that should be used for a mechanical process—entering and formatting it properly using the site's content management system—gets quickly used up by a creative one. Or the entire process gets put off until the last moment, leaving our client pulling frustrating and stressful all-nighters and becoming more resentful toward the new website they should be thrilled about using. Another comes about when new website owners attempt to avoid the procrastination scenario by hiring someone else to enter the content for them, but then find themselves disoriented and unfamiliar with their site later on.

With these pitfalls in mind, here are four simple ground rules for content entry.

1. Content Entry Is Not Content Creation

This cannot be stressed enough. Content entry is a mechanical process, not a creative one. If you have not done the creative work beforehand—writing, image creation, video and audio work, etc.—you will certainly run out of time trying to create and enter content at this point in the project. What's worse, rushed creative is always sloppy. Once you've defined personas and made some headway into prototyping during the website planning process, you should be able to start creating content. Starting then gives you ample time to do it well.

2. Don't Waste Time Styling

A well-designed and well-built website should automate as many of its design elements as possible by using site-wide CSS styling and content-specific templates, freeing its users from being overly concerned about styling during the content entry process. During the content creation process, you should simply focus on substance: what you need to say, not how big that headline will be.

3. Start as Early as Possible

You want to start using a new website as early as you can. Once the whitescreen has been built and tested, it is fully functional, which means integration can begin then, even though the visual design hasn't been applied yet. It may not look pretty, but that actually tends to help users focus on the content rather than being distracted by how things look. In some cases, though, visual functionality (like a javascript-driven slide show, for example) may not be in place until the design application process is complete. But entering slide show images should be a much faster process than entering more substantial content, like articles, blog posts and the like.

4. You Don't Need a "Moving Company"

Moving companies have clearly perfected the skills of organizing, packing and transporting household items. While individual items and homes are unique, the challenges and tools are the same from job to job, so you can trust that a mover will be able to handle getting your heirloom china from your old home to your new one in one piece. This kind of service may work wonderfully with homes, but it doesn't work very well with websites. "Moving in" to a website involves the same kind of work as using it long term, so it is to any site owner's advantage to get familiar with their new home as early and naturally as possible. If the first time you interact with your CMS is much later—say, when you're under the gun to get a press release up—it probably won't go very well. Moreover, every website has unique functionality and logic behind it, which presents an added obstacle to any third party trying to enter its content.

Launch

Unlike every other step in the web development process, the procedure of launching a new website is less about slow planning and long bouts of hard work than it is about concentrated and precise coordination. Imagine opening night of a theater production: Months of work has already been done rehearsing the actors; creating the costumes, props and set; memorizing cues; planning and testing utility flow charts for things like audio and visual effects; and promoting the show itself. In the brief span of time in which the play is actually performed, everything that has been prepared for in advance must be executed just so in order to preserve the continuity of the experience. Once that curtain begins to rise, everything is part of a precise and coordinated series of events.

Coordinating the launch of a new website is similar to a play's opening night. The site has been prototyped, designed, built, tested and used, but all on a staging server that only the project team can see. Launching the site involves moving the entire working site—its database, CMS and content—to a live server configured so that anyone who goes to the new website's address will see it in all its glory. While it may sound pretty simple, it actually involves the careful collaboration of several people on the team, typically guided by a project manager.

The first priority for the project manager coordinating launch is to confirm that the team has access to the administrative account for their website's domain name. Every web domain (i.e., website.com) has a domain name server (DNS) associated with it that needs to be correctly configured to refer site visitors to the IP address for the server where the actual site files are stored. Whoever has access to the administrative settings for the domain needs to update the domain's "A" (address) record in advance of transferring the site from its staging server to its live server. Making this change is as simple as logging in to the account and changing a few field values, but sometimes tracking down the actual username and password for this account can be difficult. I recommend gathering this information far in advance of the planned go-live date. Once the A-record is changed, the amount of time needed for the new A-record to be propagated across the web's servers is unpredictable, potentially even taking up to 48 hours for some viewers in remote locations.

During the launch procedure, the project manager should also facilitate communication between the team's members.[9] For a team spread out geographically, text and video chat tools are terrific for making sure everyone knows what the others are doing.

A systems administrator will prepare the live server in advance for the new site and assist the developer by transferring files and setting up scripts for routine automated functions, like keyword ranking trackers and scheduled data imports (i.e., inventory reconciliation). The developer, with the systems administrator's assistance, will transfer the site files from the staging server to the live server and make sure that everything he has built works properly once moved. An important detail that the developer will cover is to update configuration files that use URLs or IP addresses specific to the staging server. Without doing this critical step, many functional elements would not work properly once in place on the new server.

Going live with a new website is just the beginning. Immediately you want to have all hands on deck start using the site, just to make sure everything works as it should. This kind of post-live testing is best done by everyone involved and then some. Having as many fresh sets of eyes on a site as possible will ensure that even the smallest details don't go unnoticed. Once the site is actually being used, you'll begin to have an even clearer sense of additional things it needs to do, changes it needs and the like, which is why content strategy and the ongoing nurturing of a website are the next topics in this series.

Too Much Information!

As I hoped to indicate with the three big caveats I offered at the beginning of this section, this has only been an overview of the process. Specifically, I noted—and will no doubt mention again and again throughout the remaining chapters—that this book cannot be a singularly complete web design and development resource. There is far too much information relevant to the subject to be manageably contained by one book; indeed, each phase of the process, role and deliverable I've mentioned so far could easily have an entire book devoted to it alone. But reviewing the entire process, as we now have, is necessary to get the correct impression of the scope of the work involved in creating just one website.

Rather than let the enormity of the task tempt you to turn back, instead let it be a sober influence on how you plan your web project. The next chapter, on web personas, will cover the true object of all this planning— those for whom you're creating your website in the first place.

YOUR WEBSITE
IS NOT FOR YOU

It's easy to assume that your knowledge will be enough to guide a successful web project. But that's often not the case, which is why many web development projects I've managed in the past actually began to feel more like an interior decorating process than the carefully considered marketing initiatives they were supposed to be. Let me explain: If you were decorating your office space, it would make sense that your decision-making rubric be something like, "Can I live with this for the next few years?" Asking this same question as a means of qualifying each decision you were presented with—the kinds of desks you might use, new chairs, lighting options, wall color and the like—would maintain your focus on making choices that would support, rather than interfere with, your productivity. In that scenario, it really would be all about you. But that's precisely the point: Your website is not all about you. It's always about someone else. And yet, I've seen many teams apply the same interior decor rubric to web projects without realizing that they are not, in fact, the object of their website.

Rather than an office, which is for the most part a private work space, a website is more like a store; it should be designed for the customer, not for the shopkeepers. Sure, the shopkeeper may spend more time there on the whole—this is a reality that certainly carries over to the web, as a quick look into any website's analytics account will tell you—but the customers are the reason the shop exists in the first place. They are the object of the store, just as the intended user—not you!—is the object of your website. Reorienting to a customer or user focus is the first, albeit simple, step in avoiding what I call "project narcissism," which is my lay psychologist's diagnosis for what happens when you make the mistake of thinking that something meant for someone else is all about you. The next step, on the other hand, is less glib: to specifically identify those users as "personas" so that they may serve as guides to preserve user focus throughout the project. Developing personas is the antidote to chronic project narcissism.

The Mysterious Mind of the Audience

Your first instinct may be that if you could only ask users directly, you'd have the information you need. But just as someone building a website may have difficulty acknowledging that they are not its intended audience, someone who is will probably have difficulty imagining so realistically, especially under questioning. In a PBS *Frontline* documentary called "The Persuaders,"[1] author and correspondent Douglas Rushkoff interviewed Clotaire Rapaille, a market researcher who has built his career upon dissecting what he calls the "irrational mind" of the consumer. In one scene, Rapaille begins a lecture to a luxury marketing group by saying what might as well be his mantra: "I don't believe what people say. I want to understand why they do what they do." Rapaille's research process, which he has developed over years of practice, involves consumer focus groups that are structured to systematically filter out the rational perspective of participants in order to home in on the more instinctual—even primitive—mind that drives decisions. Rushkoff reports that many luxury brands credit Rapaille's consumer "code" with providing them with desire-prompting strategies that effectively appeal precisely to the subconscious mind, rather than the conscious one.

In the years since "The Persuaders" aired in 2004, significant changes in marketing and advertising have increased consumer awareness of how this all works. Though only slightly effective in ameliorating our general gullibility toward gurus like Rapaille, recognizably tactical advertising (e.g., the disingenuousness of pitch language and invasiveness of tracking technology) has been even more effective in demonstrating his claims. While we may want to rebel against the idea that we are collectively and individually predictable, the data gathered by technology designed to silently and invisibly follow us around the store, so to speak, repeatedly leads to the conclusion that our behaviors fall into foreseeable patterns.[2] Of course, that doesn't at all mean that consumer behavior is easily understood or predicted. In recent years, massive data analysis firms have been established solely to help us extract actionable meaning from the glut of data at our disposal, yet questions about whom the data represents still abound. In fact, "The Persuaders" constructs its main narrative around the story of Song Airlines, a short-lived subsidiary created by Delta Air Lines to compete with other low-cost carriers like JetBlue. Song's marketing executives, having rigorously employed surveys, focus groups and deep data analysis, believed that they had precisely discerned the Song persona: "Carrie" was employed, married with three children, had expensive tastes paired with practical buying habits but, most important, didn't yet "have" an airline. The assumption of brand loyalty to airlines was just one faulty premise; in hindsight, the rise of price comparison engines like Priceline. com seems to make it clear that, as far as the airline industry is concerned, consumers are primarily loyal to fare—no matter what they may say.

Yet, a default skepticism toward what consumers say is no better a position than ignorance. You may gain the ground in your understanding of the limitations of consumer feedback, but until you figure out how to discover what drives behavior, you will lack the insight you need to create meaningful and useful experiences on the web. We need to expand our perspective through discourse with consumers; we have to ask questions. That's obvious. The key is to ask the right questions.

In 2009, Walmart learned that lesson the hard way.[3] After conducting a survey that asked if customers would prefer that Walmart's aisles be less "cluttered" and receiving an overwhelming affirmative in response, they implemented a large-scale inventory reduction program. It seems obvious in hindsight that fewer items for sale would lead to fewer sales, but executives were enamored enough with the prospect of giving customers what they wanted to suspend critical thinking at a, well, critical juncture. The flaw here was not in asking the customer questions and taking action on the basis of their answers. The problem was in the question itself. First, it was a leading question. No records of customer data showed that a significant population already held the opinion that Walmart's aisles were cluttered. In framing the question around a word with such a negative connotation, it seems clearly unlikely that a majority would have answered in the negative. Who wouldn't prefer a less-cluttered space? Had Walmart asked if customers would prefer that less inventory be made available in the aisles, again, it seems quite unlikely that a majority would have answered "yes." For Walmart, the cost of asking the wrong question turned out to be over $1 billion in lost sales. Thankfully, our web-based stakes are almost assuredly lower, but the principle also scales as low as you need it to. If you really want actionable information from your customers, your questions need to be carefully considered and bleached of any assumptions you might already have.

Web Persona Development

If, as makers of websites, we have an inherent inclination toward narcissism, and as consumers, a certain lack of true self-awareness, it would seem that an insurmountable psychological barrier exists between us and the clarity we need to create effective web marketing experiences. But that is not entirely the case; there are, of course, specific methods for creating conditions under which observation can retrieve legitimate, actionable insights. I'd like to briefly review two of those methods: web persona development and conditioned usability testing.

Steve Mulder, author of *The User Is Always Right*[4], defines a web persona as follows:

A realistic personality profile that represents a significant group of your website's users.

Even though creating consumer personas has been a common marketing practice for decades—one with which you may even have direct experience—applying the same principles to website planning tends to be overlooked. But without going through the process of web persona development, you're much more prone to making guesses (at best) or assumptions (at worst) about who the audience of your website actually is. In most cases, your guesses/assumptions will really look more like you than anyone else. Creating web personas, whether they are specific, general or behavioral, prevents us from mistakenly building websites for ourselves rather than those we want to serve.

Depending upon the particular type of assessment process you use, identifying specific personas for a website could take a significant amount of time. In fact, if you follow Mulder's most rigorous process, it could take months. If you have the resources and the investment seems prudent given your project, I'd certainly recommend reading his book and following his process to the letter. If you don't have that kind of time, a simplified, abridged process should at least involve a series of interviews with employees and clients and ultimately produce several unique profiles. This also would be a good time to involve sales personnel, if your website is representing a product or service around which a sales team and process has been defined. Because they're on the front lines, they probably have an even clearer idea of who the audience—especially the buying audience—is.

However you approach it, a persona diagnostic will help you focus on what really matters for the project, rather than on what you might be inclined to think matters. If you don't have the time or resources to do a persona discovery phase at all, you can still weave the basic concept into your process by focusing on general and behavioral personas as you plan and design the website itself (more on that later).

If you do decide to try creating some specific web personas, I recommend creating three to five profiles, focusing on what Mulder calls "qualitative" assessment—akin to creating a story about your persona—rather than a quantitative one, which results in a large and often unnecessarily peripheral data set. From start to finish, a qualitative approach will probably take you two to four weeks, whereas a quantitative approach could easily take twice that amount of time without representing a significant value gain to you in this planning process. Creating qualitatively driven web personas involves a four-step process of research, segmentation, creation and testing.

To properly research personas, you'll want to conduct one-on-one phone interviews with a group of active and valued clients, as well as prospects familiar with your company. These interviews should follow a standardized routine that provides a base structure (especially for the purposes of maintaining a time limit; remember, your interviewees have generously offered you precious moments of their day) upon which you can informally explore the feedback you receive.

I personally conducted a series of persona development interviews for my firm early in 2011. While my first few sessions felt a bit too rigid, with me woodenly sticking to the script and hesitant to wander into more obscure territory, I eventually grew more accustomed to the process and confident in my ability to improvise questions more keenly crafted to each situation. Having a colleague join me to listen and take notes was essential to my ability to both focus on having a natural conversation that covered the goals, attitudes and behaviors of the interviewee as well as keep from veering too far off course. So, of course, I recommend inviting into the process someone whom you can trust to set you at ease and be a good scribe. Once you've completed your interviews, you'll need to begin translating your interviewees into three to five segments. Having the perspective of your observer to balance out your subjective recall of the interviews will, again, be indispensable, as segmenting personas is an intuitive, rather than scientific, process. Its goal is to generalize your personas and qualify them for uniqueness, realism, describability, user-base coverage and influence upon the decisions you will make about your website. Remember, the purpose of this exercise is to go beyond learning *about* your users in order to learn *from* them.

Each segment should be represented by a unique, yet paradigmatic persona, documented by a profile card. A profile card can be designed to look any way you wish, but it should include basic identifiers, like a name, description and photo of a representative user. Rather than only referring to your personas by actual names from your interviewee pool, like Song's "Carrie," also include a simplified description indicative of their behavior. For example, you might name a persona representing someone who thoroughly vets content sources in order to help influence buying decisions made by a superior "Brian, the Analytical Influencer." Your persona profiles should also include a longer description that focuses on what that person values and how they make decisions, as well as some personal information that fills in enough backstory to provide likely and understandable motives. Precision here is more important than accuracy. In other words, a thorough but realistic description is more important to your decision making than whether the description actually applies to the person upon whom you've based your persona.

Finally, to test your personas, use and act out decision-making scenarios. A basic testing scenario might start with a search engine query for a description of your service or product (no specific names, though—we're acting as people who don't yet know about you) and follow the path from landing on your site's home page to finding a low-level detail page and responding to a call to action. If you construct your site to allow for this kind of procedure, you'll make better choices as to the types of content and calls to action that would be available based upon your personas.

As I alluded to earlier, you don't have to go "all the way" through a persona development process in order to start improving an existing website or one further along in the development process. Adopting the points of view of simpler, general web personas can do a great deal to make your website more effective.

For the most part, general web personas can be divided into two basic types: "decision makers" and "influencers." Most specific web personas are going to be decision makers—the type of person who is looking to buy a product or service. These are the people who are looking for a solution that addresses an immediate problem and are looking to implement it soon. For decision makers, key facts, specific benefits, pricing and clear calls to action that will begin the purchasing process are going to be essential.

On the other hand, influencers are the research-oriented users who are gathering information in order to help make a decision that is usually a bit farther off. Some might just be enthusiasts who will, some day, be in a decision-making position. For influencers, informational content—whether from blogs, articles, whitepapers, webinars or customer forums—and clear calls to action—to subscribe to various content channels or register for events—are going to be critical in engaging their long-term interest.

Finally, it would be wise to also consider two basic behavioral personas when planning the information architecture of a website. These are very simple: Some users are browsing oriented and will tend toward exploring a website's menus in order to gain an understanding of its contents, while others are search oriented and will almost immediately use a website's search tools in order to determine if it contains what they are looking for. These personas are independent of any industry or genre, so you need to enable the website you are working on to be friendly to both.

Conditioned Usability Testing

While developing personas can be extremely effective in proactively homing in on the user's desires and needs, even well-developed ones won't result in a flawless website. The truth is there are no perfect launches. Actually, like "the web is a permanent work in progress," this should become a motto you repeat to yourself and others often. It's appropriate that we refer to launching a new website as "going live"; a "live" website begins to change radically and rapidly once it starts being used, which demands ongoing maintenance: bug fixes, design tweaks, functionality changes and the like. This has certainly been true in my experience. After launching a new site in January of 2010, my firm anticipated a focused round of work at some point later, perhaps a year or so after launch—what we often refer to as a "Phase 2." Though we had been consistently maintaining our site since its relaunch, we often discovered flaws that we just would not have been able to anticipate until it began to be used, and so we added them to our list of Phase 2 items. I recount all of this to answer what I can imagine might be anyone's response to the kinds of things usability tests often reveal: "Why didn't you build it that way in the first place?" The answer is simpler to say than it is to experience, but I assure you that the reality is sound: You can build a website with all the intelligence, care, earnestness and good intentions possible, but you will find that some of your decisions were good guesses later proven wrong.

One of the wonderful things about the web is that it is interwoven with the people who create and use it, making it an organic entity and environment that is just as unpredictable as the rest of our lives so clearly are. Our job is to continually adapt what we do and how we do it as we learn new things by observation—it's all a work in progress. So, moving on: Usability tests will reveal better ways of doing things that you've already spent time and money doing differently. It's OK; that's exactly what they're for.

Before we began actually plugging away at our Phase 2 list, we decided to take a step back and investigate—through usability testing of some kind—whether our assessment was a good enough measure of what was working about our website and what was not. We sincerely wanted to know how we could improve our site for the people who use it, but we didn't relish the thought of mounting a long and expensive process to get there. Fortunately we had an established model to follow provided by our old friend, Steve Krug, of *Don't Make Me Think* fame. Krug's most recent book, *Rocket Surgery Made Easy: The Do-It-Yourself Guide to Finding and Fixing Usability Problems*,[5] provides a fantastic overview of how to do usability testing in a way that provides fast and valuable results. If you're interested in usability testing for web projects, I'd heartily recommend the book; it definitely belongs on every interactive designer's bookshelf. After our entire team read it, we regrouped and distilled Krug's advice down to a simple three-step process that can be replicated for just about any website and run in about ten minutes or less. Before I specify the steps, though, I'd like to offer a caveat: This is a basic procedure; Krug provides and recommends much more. On its own, it will certainly provide plenty of insight, but it could easily be expanded upon to test more complex functionality.

Keep in mind, though, that what you're not doing here is simply observing people using your website. An unfocused situation like that is only likely to compound the sense of confusion you probably have at the outset. As we learned from the Walmart example, any diagnostic procedure, whether it be to develop and test personas or to run usability tests on a working website, should begin with specific questions that are answered with specific procedures catered to those questions.

Step 1: Customizing the Test

Since you now know that sitting volunteers in front of a website and recording their browsing patterns is not usability testing, your first step is to customize the test—to plan its steps specifically around the goals of the website you want to evaluate. The framework of the kind of testing I'm recommending is pretty basic. First, have your volunteers spend a few moments (one or two maximum) simply orienting themselves on the website's home page, feeling free to narrate their observations as they do. You'll want to ask that they not click any links that navigate away from the home page but just observe what it contains (scrolling is OK) and then explain to the moderator what they perceive the website to be about. While many volunteers may have difficulty comprehending the purpose of an especially tightly positioned site, the goal of the orientation is to observe how well the home page communicates the website's purpose—even if the user may not understand what it means. For example, if a volunteer rightly concludes that a website offers "industrial plastics extrusion equipment," you could give the site points for clarity even if the volunteer doesn't know what "industrial plastics extrusion equipment" is.

The rest of the test should be based upon three or four specific tasks that you would assign to your volunteer. Each task should correspond to specific goals of the website and test the user's ability to complete those goals. These goals could include subscribing to content, registering for events, requesting more information or making a purchase, as long as they target the primary purpose of the site. For example, a test for a website similar to the one my firm maintains—which relies heavily upon a written content strategy and has corresponding sign-up calls to action—should include at least one task in which the volunteer must find a specific article and sign up to receive that content.

Step 2: Administering the Test

Ideally, your volunteer should be someone who has little to no familiarity with the website you are testing. That means that the designer, developer, planner, account executive, client and CEO need not apply. Anyone else, theoretically, is qualified. By the way, since you're only going to be asking for a few minutes of this person's time, *volunteer* is certainly still an appropriate word, though it couldn't hurt to reward them for their effort—a Starbucks gift card, lunch on you, anything big enough to say "thank you" but small enough to not be a budget barrier for you. And about those ten minutes—try to have everything set up before your volunteer arrives so you can keep it as short as possible. That should really amount to turning the computer on, loading the site in an uncluttered browser and opening up whatever screen-capture software you've chosen to use to record the session.

Once your volunteer is comfortable, go ahead and start recording. Take them slowly and clearly through each test question, starting with the home page orientation, being careful not to lead them to any conclusions. Remember, words (like *cluttered*) that are obviously weighted positive or negative should not be used. Feel free to ask clarifying or expanding questions—things like, "What's happening here?" "Can you say more about that?" or "What was difficult about that?"—but nothing specific enough to transfer any suspicions or biases you already have. Remember, that's why you are not sitting where the volunteer is. You've lost the objectivity they have. It helps to have a hard copy of your test questions on which you can write notes during the test. Even though the video will capture everything your volunteer does, it may not clearly demonstrate other things you observe. If your volunteer gets stuck for too long on any of your two or three tasks, that's probably an indicator that something isn't working—either with the site or the test—and it is probably a good time to move on. You'll find that the briefer the test, the more productive.

Step 3. Evaluating the Test Results

On its own, observing your volunteers will likely produce plenty of insight as to what is not working on your website. But as the process itself is controlled and systematic, it doesn't hurt to be a bit more methodical in your evaluation of the data you've gathered. Each of your testing sessions should have produced a roughly five-minute video clip. After you've administered all the sessions (somewhere between five and ten would be wise), go through each one and assemble a list of takeaways from each task, then consolidate the points from each session into one master list. Once you've done that, I'd recommend assembling your development team—all the people I said were not qualified to be volunteers—to watch the videos, review your master list and brainstorm solutions together.

I began this chapter by referring to the mind of the audience as mysterious. In some ways, that is certainly the case. Human beings are unique and can be quite unpredictable. But on the other hand, people do want to be known, especially when that results in experiences and products that more closely fit their needs. That, really, is the point of all this—to better know so that we may better serve. Beginning with pinpointing what you don't know, which always leads to asking the right questions, you can apply the persona and usability systems I've outlined with reasonable expectations and a much higher likelihood of success.

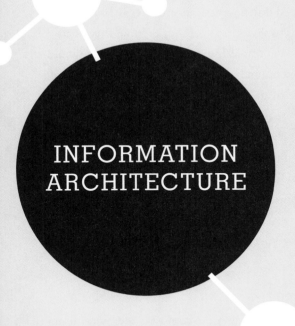

INFORMATION
ARCHITECTURE

Since the beginning of the web, many approaches have been taken to plan the structure and information architecture of websites that are, on the whole, ineffective. You've no doubt seen or perhaps even used these methods yourself. Two in particular—site maps and wireframes—are still in wide employ as the primary planning documents for many web projects, despite being woefully inadequate for the task. Before I describe the best method of website information architecture planning, I'd like to first describe site maps and wireframes and explain why they're not quite up to task.

Site Maps

A site map is simply an outline of the pages a website will contain. Think about what information an outline actually provides. If the content of this book, for example, were reduced down to the outline I began with, you would have an overview of the subjects it covers, but the majority of its insight and value to you would be lost. While the word *prototyping* would certainly be listed, without the content represented by that headline you'd be at a loss to explain the value of prototyping or how to create one. Now imagine you had the outline I created for this book project before I began writing. That outline would likely be substantially different from an outline "reverse engineered" from the finished manuscript. This is because an initial outline, as all site maps created for planning purposes are, is an impression of a website's structure and content that has not been tested by actual web-based interaction. As a planning method, they are fine places to start—like a cocktail napkin might be for logo designs—but nothing more.

Wireframes

So what about wireframes? Albeit slightly more sophisticated, wireframes are just as ineffective a website planning method as site maps. If you're unfamiliar with what a wireframe is, imagine a web page reduced to a two-dimensional linear drawing on paper—almost like a blueprint. Rather than specifics, wireframes might generalize things and substitute generic filler copy for the content that will eventually occupy the page as a way to preserve the conceptual limitations of the planning phase as if to say, "these pages are telling you how things will work, not how they'll look." But the result tends to be much more confusing than helpful. Imagine reviewing a set of wireframes for even a modestly sized website. You'd potentially have twenty to thirty pages tacked up on the wall, perhaps arranged in a way that indicates an assumed flow of use. Without being able to observe actual use, that flow would be no more than an assumption, and probably a very incorrect one at that. As far as realistic use is concerned, a wireframe will not provide any insight. All you can really do is look at it.

Communicating Experiences

The information you need from the planning stage is necessarily tied to use. Site maps and wireframes—two-dimensional, paper documents— are incapable of communicating anything even remotely close to the experience of using a website. After all, they are translating an interactive experience through a static medium. All kinds of metaphors can expose the absurdity of this. But one that emphasized this point for me recently came after a visit to the American Museum of Natural History, one of my favorite places to visit in New York.

Among its permanent collection is a series of dioramas[1] depicting animals of all kinds in their natural habitats. I could spend hours looking at these works of art; they are beautiful and astonishing in their detail and care. But despite all that detail, they leave out more than they contain.

As I stood and gazed at one in particular[2]—two brown bears, one standing, the other on all fours considering the trout it had just pulled from a nearby stream; the dirt of the small shore; the golden plains grass around them; and of course the snowcapped Alaskan mountains far in the distance behind them—I realized that everything else I was experiencing—the dry cold air, the gurgling of the river, the smell of the grass and dirt and the fear of these menacing, powerful predators—was filled in by my imagination. Yet, it was this content—the visceral, sensory information—that provided the experience by infusing it with meaning. Triggered by the symbols depicted in the diorama, I invented the experience for myself, which will remain true to me until I set foot on the actual soil of the Alaskan Brown Bear's habitat and am corrected by reality.

This is exactly what happens, though certainly with less excitement, with wireframes. They attempt to capture the essence of a website in a frozen and generalized format, leaving the viewer to fill the rest in with his imagination. But that's what should really scare you: If everyone lets their imagination supply the experience, then everyone will expect a different website. No website built from such general specifications will satisfy anyone's expectations, even the realistic ones! So, if paper site maps and wireframes are no good for website planning, what is?[3]

Prototyping

Website prototyping involves the creation of an interactive experience that effectively communicates the structure, information and functionality of a website in a way that enables the remaining steps in the process, specifically design and development, to proceed without the possibility of emerging on the other side with contradictory results. Essentially, prototyping means building a model of the website before you build the actual website. Of course, from a developmental standpoint, a prototype isn't actually built in the same way that a sophisticated website would be. A simple prototype might be a collection of clickable HTML pages that describe more complex, database-driven functionality—for example, by depicting the results of a search rather than actually receiving and processing queries—without being concerned with design-related issues of look and feel, colors, typography, images and the like.

At my firm, we call these prototypes "grayscreens"[4] to emphasize the lack of design and focus our clients' attention on the kinds of decision making that really matter at this stage in the process. Namely how the website will be structured, what specific pages will be included, the specific functionality they contain and a general sense of the layout of information on each page. While we use a proprietary system to construct these prototypes, there are

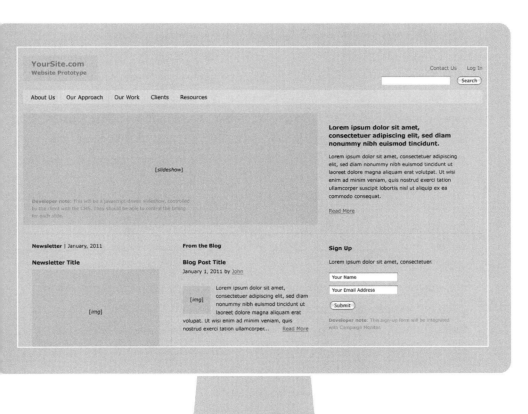

A good prototype, like the "grayscreen" shown above, should work just like a real website, allowing the user to click from page to page rather than forcing them to imagine a future interactive experience.

many online tools available[5] that will enable you to construct something very similar.

In the past, I often would describe a website prototype as a plan for how a website works, not how it looks. While, in a sense, I still think that's true, I've come to realize that this distinction is actually rather confusing, don't you think? Especially since we go on and on about how site maps and wireframes are inadequate website planning techniques because they can't be experienced interactively, like a website. But a very big part of the web experience is visual! Every aspect of a website's structure and functionality is represented in some visual way by its prototype. With that in mind, it's much easier to see how the distinction between prototyping and design is fuzzier than I'd thought.

So, to better describe what exactly a website prototype is, I'd like to start by drawing a pretty simple analogy: Just as architectural plans use a consistent visual language to describe buildings, prototypes use a consistent visual language to describe websites. In both cases, there are many good reasons for the consistency part. Architects are trained to read plans and discern critical specifications from them that are later translated into three-dimensional structures. Likewise, website developers are trained to interpret prototypes and translate their specifications into functional code. You could say that the use of conventions make the plans look very similar, but that doesn't stop the results from being quite distinct.

For designers, rather than seeing the prototype as a document that imposes limitations, I think it makes more sense to see it as one that enables creative freedom. Believe me, I'm not trying to spin this. To milk my architecture analogy just a bit more, imagine if blueprints didn't exist. Without them, it would be remarkable to see buildings constructed at all, but it would be even more amazing if the ones that were built remained standing! In the same way, prototypes provide a structure that ensures a website is even possible. No matter how attractive a design might be, if it is not possible, it is useless.

Essentially what I'm saying is that a good prototype wants to support good design, not step on its toes. But I realize I'm going to have to get a bit

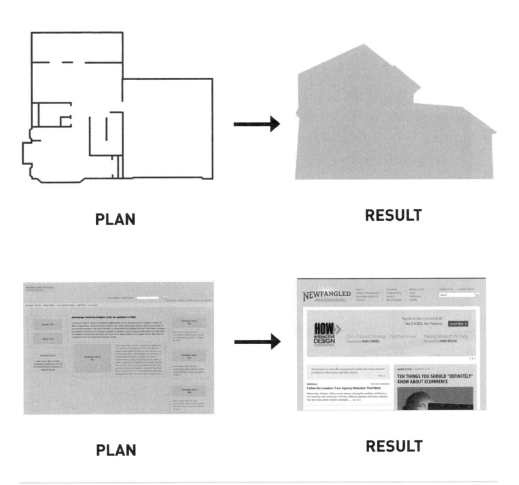

PLAN

RESULT

PLAN

RESULT

Website prototypes serve as plans for the construction of a working website, just as blueprints do for buildings.

more into the details of how prototypes communicate in order to build my case, so bear with me.

The Language of Prototypes

The first priority of a prototype is to accurately represent the information a website will contain. That includes structural information—like the hierarchy of pages and subpages that make up a website—as well as content, which includes everything from the words and images displayed on pages to the logic behind content relationships and other functionality. In other words, a prototype has a big, big job: communicating a ton of technical information that will be understandable to everyone involved in the project—the technical and the nontechnical—without using technical language (or for that matter, even working at all). Let me explain ...

At the time of this writing, sunrise is expected about fifteen hours from now. Maybe if I'm still up then (working on this chapter, of course), I'll stop for a break and watch the sun come up. But, probably not. The reason I bring up sunrise is that it's a perfect example of phenomenological language,[6] which is exactly the kind of language a prototype uses. If you speak prototype—which I hope you will by the end of this article—you speak phenomenologically, which is to say, you speak in a way that describes experiences. We know that the sun doesn't actually rise, but from our subjective vantage point way down here on Earth, it looks like it does. The Earth would have to be much, much smaller in order for us to experience its day-long spin. So, despite our modern enlightenment, we still say "sunrise" because it's a whole lot clearer (and less pedantic) than saying "the time in the morning when we've spun around enough to see the sun again."

Prototypes describe what it will be like to use a website—that's the phenomenological part—in a way that satisfactorily engages and prepares the client, without confusing anyone with overly technical jargon. But that begs the question, if the prototype doesn't use technical language, how does a developer know what to build?

To answer that, let me first show you an example of a prototype:

Contact Us   Log In

[Search]

About Us   Our Approach   Our Work   Clients   Resources

[slideshow]

Developer note: This will be a javascript-driven slideshow, controlled
by the client with the CMS. They should be able to control the timing
for each slide.

**Lorem ipsum dolor sit amet,
consectetuer adipiscing elit, sed diam
nonummy nibh euismod tincidunt.**

Lorem ipsum dolor sit amet, consectetuer adipiscing
elit, sed diam nonummy nibh euismod tincidunt ut
laoreet dolore magna aliquam erat volutpat. Ut wisi
enim ad minim veniam, quis nostrud exerci tation
ullamcorper suscipit lobortis nisl ut aliquip ex ea
commodo consequat.

Read More

Newsletter | January, 2011

Newsletter Title

[img]

Lorem ipsum dolor sit amet, consectetuer adipiscing
elit, sed diam nonummy nibh euismod tincidunt ut
laoreet dolore magna aliquam erat volutpat. Ut wisi
enim ad minim veniam, quis nostrud exerci tation
ullamcorper suscipit lobortis nisl ut aliquip ex ea
commodo consequat...   Read More

From the Blog

Blog Post Title
January 1, 2011 by John

[img]   Lorem ipsum dolor sit amet,
           consectetuer adipiscing elit, sed diam
           nonummy nibh euismod tincidunt ut
           laoreet dolore magna aliquam erat
volupat. Ut wisi enim ad minim veniam, quis
nostrud exerci tation ullamcorper...   Read More

Blog Post Title
January 1, 2011 by John

[img]   Lorem ipsum dolor sit amet,
           consectetuer adipiscing elit, sed diam
           nonummy nibh euismod tincidunt ut
           laoreet dolore magna aliquam erat
volupat. Ut wisi enim ad minim veniam, quis
nostrud exerci tation ullamcorper...   Read More

Sign Up

Lorem ipsum dolor sit amet, consectetuer.

Your Name

Your Email Address

Submit

Developer note: This sign-up form will be integrated
with Campaign Monitor.

© 2011 Your Company | New York, NY | 800-123-4567
Lorem ipsum dolor sit amet, consectetuer adipiscing elit, sed diam nonummy nibh euismod tincidunt ut
laoreet dolore magna aliquam erat volutpat.

The first thing you probably noticed is that the prototype is mostly gray (hence "grayscreen"). This is intentional, to make sure that nobody gets sidetracked by any aesthetic hang-ups. At this point, you're not interested in whether the prototype is pretty, just whether or not it works. The second thing you may have noticed is that the prototype looks like a website. Well, sort of. The page is certainly laid out like a website would be (and, were this an actual prototype, you could navigate from one page to another), but some things are specific while others are generic. For instance, the main navigation has what looks like specific page names in it, but other parts of the page have generic titles like "Blog Post Title."

These are the brass tacks of the language of prototypes. In general, some aspects of the site will be very specific and the way the prototype describes them will reflect that. So, from this image, the main pages (and their subpages) are named, and though that doesn't necessarily mean those names cannot be changed once the website is built, they're probably not likely to do so very often. On the other hand, the blog post that is featured on the home page is likely to change very often. By using generic language, as opposed to prototyping a specific blog post title, the prototype is communicating to the developer that the site should be built in such a way that the end user can add new blog posts and name them whatever they wish. Just like "lorem ipsum" dummy text generally means "text will be here," generic titles stand in for types of content that are meant to be editable.

The Sequence of Prototyping

The order in which you actually build a prototype may be, in some places, somewhat counterintuitive. Let me first outline the five main prototyping stages and then explain each one in a bit more detail.

Stage 1 involves identifying the overall page structure of the website and arranging pages within navigation menus in order to make them all intuitively accessible to users and indexable by search engines.

Next, in Stage 2, the key landing pages should begin to take shape. More than simply accounting for them in the structure of the site, this stage

DESIGN

PROTOTYPE

A prototype is aesthetically agnostic and can lead to a variety of visual outcomes.

should involve specifically outlining the information that these pages will provide and organizing it within a usable template.

Stage 3 is similar to the previous one, but rather than focusing on key informational pages, you should now devote your attention to those pages containing supporting content. Supporting content is the material your content strategy has planned for—newsletters, whitepapers, case studies, blogs, videos and the like.

Once you've completed Stages 1 through 3, finalizing the majority of the website's pages and content types, you need to identify the calls to action that your website will include in Stage 4 and begin to associate individual ones to the specific pages where they will be most appropriate. You should also spend some time outlining a functional work flow for how the website's content management system will enable its administrators to flexibly control the placement of calls to action as the site grows.

Stage 5 is focused only on your website's home page. Since you've identified the structure of the site, its content and how it will engage with users, a sense of priority should now be clear and help to make home page content decisions simple.

Finally, Stage 6 is reserved for specifying the search and filtering tools that your website will provide users. This is intentionally left until the end in order to make sure that the content determines the tools rather than the other way around.

The Structure of Prototype Pages

Actually articulating how pages work, which is the heart of prototyping, and relevant to each of the six stages I listed above, is where I think most of the fuzziness between prototyping and design comes into play. Because the prototype must communicate the website experience (that phenomenological language again), it has to work like a website—which means you need to be able to click from page to page. But in order to work like a website, it has to look like one, too. That's why I began this chapter by discussing how site maps (in that they don't look or work like a website) and wireframes (in that they look in a Flatland kind of way like websites but don't work like them) fail to communicate anything useful about, well, using websites. Where I'm heading with this is all about the "looking" part is that since prototypes need to look like websites, they can't look just any way. The honest truth is that building a prototype does involve a kind of design.

The kind of design I'm talking about has to do with communicating the priority of information on a page—or, to put it simply, information design. Information design, as it pertains to web pages, is an enormous topic that I certainly cannot cover in depth in this chapter alone. With humility, I'd rather defer to Steve Krug and recommend his book *Don't Make Me Think*[7] as the best source on the topic. (Everyone involved in web work of any kind should own it.) But for now, and with all the caveats required of such simplification, I will summarize the role of information design in creating an effective prototype as returning to two core principles over and over again with every information design decision that the team makes:

1. What is the purpose of the website?

2. For whom are we building it?

The answers to those questions should lead to very focused pages with a clear sense of priority. This is often manifest in visual decisions—such as the relative sizes and positions of elements on a page or typographical details, if the volume of information on a page warrants it. Let me unpack this with another example:

Though the example of a prototyped home page on page 71 has a very deliberate layout in which the information on the page has been clearly and intentionally ordered, the spectrum of possibilities for how the final website can look is still quite broad.

Each visual design example takes liberties with elements of the page, but neither removes essential information nor disrupts the order of the information in a way that fundamentally changes the focus of the page. The interactive slide show element, for example, which occupies about three-fourths of the horizontal space at the top of the page, is still the most prominent visual element in both designs, even though Option 1 has made it slightly wider. The sign-up form, too, has not been fundamentally affected, though in Option 2 it is relocated to the left side of the page. Nor has the choice to limit the number of blog posts aggregated on Option 2's home page significantly altered the overall priority of blog content on the page. Aside from these specific layout choices, Option 1 and Option 2 represent very different creative directions without undermining the integrity or violating the intent of the prototype.

Designing Navigation Menus

Navigation menus are probably the most important user experience tool a website has to offer, which is why it makes sense to first resolve a website's structure before proceeding with a prototype.

Without menus, most websites would be unnavigable—leaving vast amounts of content simply unreachable to users. Even if a page contained enough links in the content to make it possible to reach every other page on the website, it would lack the clarity and consistency offered by a structured, globally available navigation system. Depending upon how a navigation system is constructed, a user could potentially get an overview of all the pages and topics a website contains without actually clicking anything. For browsing-oriented users, an important persona group explained in chapter 3, way-finding provided by navigation systems is critical to the productivity of their experience.

Usability studies have continually affirmed that the conventions you are probably used to—horizontal navigation bars with interactive, vertical submenus—are highly effective and usable as they scale in complexity.[8] This is precisely why that style of navigation is the default for our prototypes. But that doesn't mean that every site must necessarily employ that style of navigation menu. Many contemporary websites, especially those without a deep enough structure to merit something more complex, are beginning to use simple list structures, for instance, rather than the standard horizontal navigation with drop-down menus.

Rather than employ too much custom programming of its own, a prototype can preserve the standard menu approach but include a note to the developer working on the project describing how the design will alter the final menu interface. As long as the conceptual structure of the website—its top pages and their subpages—isn't fundamentally changed, the interface is certainly negotiable.

Subpage Templates

In the past, a typical web design project would involve the design of a home page template and maybe one or two subpage templates that would be used for the majority of the website's content. Today, the number of uniquely designed templates is growing as our understanding of persona-based user interfaces (and overall sophistication of approach) increases. Specifying unique templates shouldn't wait for the design process, though. This should happen during the prototyping process as well. In fact, a typical prototype today can include anywhere from thirty to fifty unique pages. That's quite a lot when you consider that you have to prototype an example of a blog detail page only once!

But even unique pages can share the same layout. The point to emphasize here, again, is purpose. What is the page for? What information needs to be on the page in order to make it successful? As you work your way down, so to speak, in a website's structure, subpages should become more and more focused. A third-level page in a website's overall hierarchy—naturally more of an endpoint in a user's flow than something higher up—should provide fewer, more specific options. That means that top-level landing pages—those that provide overviews of product families, service offerings and the like—will tend to be much broader topically and, consequently, a greater information design challenge. Those pages, just like the home page, should be prototyped as specifically as possible in order to ensure that the information design problems are being solved before the visual design process starts.

Repositioning Page Elements

Your approach to forms during the prototyping process should be similar to your default approach to navigation menus—to follow established conventions that ensure the most stable user experience possible.[9] Because heat map studies continue to affirm left-to-right F-shaped user patterns on web pages,[10] form widgets are most commonly placed on the upper right-hand portion of web pages. It's a bit of a chicken-and-egg scenario, actually. Since content-related tools and resources are typically found on the right side of web pages, users intuitively return to that location as they read through pages. So, it makes sense to continue to place utilities in that space. But just because the convention is securely rooted in usability data doesn't mean there will never be good cause to do something different.

I imagine that as we continue to learn more about how to make forms and other calls to action more user focused, the convention will surely be tested and perhaps fundamentally changed. Meanwhile, implementing these kinds of touch points in the mobile context will also generate a feedback loop that will begin to shape behavior in other contexts, especially back on our desktops. That will be a trend to watch.

Other Details to Consider Sooner Than Later

Aside from the confusion around how a page's structure should be interpreted and handled by designers, there are a couple of other minor details I wanted to point out that are often easily overlooked in that fuzzy place between prototyping and design.

The first has to do with how different areas of a website will expand to fit changing content. Remember, if your website is using a CMS (I really hope it is) or will use a CMS (I really hope it will), the content on just about every page of your site is likely to change. But as powerful as a CMS is, it can't change graphical elements on the fly. Imagine a sidebar that you've designed to have an uneven edge. In your composition file, it looks great, but as soon as the content is actually changing and growing, you're likely to have a problem. How will that area stretch to fit? For dynamic content areas like this, the best approach is to keep jagged areas limited to the fixed portions—often the top and bottom—and design the flexible ones to have background images that can repeat as the vertical space expands.

The second also has to do with background graphics: those that fill the browser window behind your website's main content area. Using unique images here, as opposed to solid colors, can be a great way to add space and mood to your design, but you want to make sure that your images are wide enough to fill even the largest possible horizontal resolution or have an edge treatment that enables them to gracefully fade to a solid color or texture. Even if you have created background imagery that does anticipate wider screen resolutions, try to make the transitions as subtle as possible.

Managing the Prototyping Process

In chapter 2, I shared that the average prototype built by my firm required just under two months of production time—1.75 months was the exact figure I provided—from start to approval. I also mentioned, though, that the average amount of time logged by the development team (everyone but the client) was fifty-one hours. That works out to an average of 7.3 hours logged per week, based upon how we manage website prototyping. However, because the way my firm works is uniquely suited to many factors not generally applicable—such as efficiencies that are the result of developing around a proprietary CMS—I'd actually recommend planning for more time than that.

The team assembled to create a website prototype should include at least three people—a project manager, a designer and a developer—who will each log time against the process. (One should be in charge of actually building the prototype; whether that involves the manipulation of code or not will depend upon the tool or platform being used. At my firm, our project managers have the skills to carry out this role, allowing us to otherwise fully allocate our developers toward post-prototype production work.) If the team convenes twice each week to review the prototype—say, for an hour each time (totaling six hours)—and allocates another hour for production time in-between each review (plus two more), eight hours could potentially be spent each week. The total number of weeks required to complete the prototype would, of course, depend upon the scope of the project. The data I have gathered is pertinent to the types of projects my firm takes on, which I would estimate to be of midlevel complexity compared with websites on a spectrum of simple informational sites (aka brochureware) to larger, retail e-commerce sites (i.e., Target.com).

OPTIMIZING
CONTENT FOR
SEARCHERS

Arthur C. Clarke once wrote that "any sufficiently advanced technology is indistinguishable from magic,"[1] an insight that sheds a great deal of light on why our historical predecessors, without access to much of the knowledge we take for granted today, believed some of what they did. But it also applies to contemporary technologies, some of which we depend upon greatly yet understand only in part (or perhaps not at all).

The evolution of the meaning and use of the word *Google*—from proper noun to verb—corresponds with the increasing disconnect between web users and search technology. Ten years ago, searching for content on the web was a difficult process, but today one has only to enter a few words into Google's search bar, and Presto! (magical incantation intended): instant and accurate results. As much as this might seem like magic, it is a thoroughly mundane—albeit ingenious—technology at work. But if search engine technology is indistinguishable from magic, the process of optimizing web content for search engines will seem just as mysterious. Unfortunately it's difficult to trust what we don't understand, and mistrust breeds the very kind of problems that are rampant in the search engine optimization industry: myths, abuses and profit for those who would rather be seen as magicians than marketers.

Fortunately we know enough about how search engines work to optimize our content with words, not wands. While there is some value in examining the myths and abuses of search engine optimization (SEO), I think it makes sense to first explore how it works. I'll start with a brief explanation of how search engines (I'll focus on Google) work and then explain how web content can be optimized for them. Knowing how SEO, in its most basic form, really works will shed some light on the misunderstandings that often get in the way of doing it well.

How Google Works

Ultimately Google's purpose is to index and rank web content in order to help searchers find what they are looking for. While this is done, in part, by organizing pages on the basis of authority, the goal of Google's increasingly sophisticated algorithm is to understand the particular queries users submit—which are more likely to be specific than general, like "synthetic insulation shell" rather than "coat"—in order to direct them to the best source for the information they need. I like the way Alexis Madrigal put it in an *Atlantic Monthly* article from 2010.[2] While he was writing primarily about online matchmaking, I think he gets right at the heart of what Google is all about without being too technical:

> If only you could Google your way to The One. The search engine, in its own profane way, is a kadosh generator. Its primary goal is to find the perfect web page for you out of all the web pages in the world, to elevate it to No. 1.

So how does Google know which pages are the most authoritative? Actually Google outsources some of this work to us. Google's PageRank algorithm (named for co-founder Larry Page) took an entirely new approach in ranking pages purely on the basis of incoming links, rather than calculating the frequency of keywords within a page's content in order to discern which web pages were authoritative on any given subject. What this means is that the more important a website is—the more incoming links it has—the more influential its outgoing links will be. So a link from the *New York Times* website, which has a PageRank of 9/10, will have a greater influence over the PageRank of the site being linked to than one from a local news source, like wral.com, which has a PageRank of 7.[3]

But PageRank is only one piece of the authority puzzle. Because it is primarily concerned with scoring a website based upon the volume of its incoming links, PageRank isn't as much an indicator of authority over a particular subject as it is authority in general, so let's call that "influence" instead. And this differentiation is really for the best. After all, even though the *New York Times* is a nationally trusted news source, you probably wouldn't expect them to be a better source for information on SEO than, say, my firm's website—even though Newfangled.com's PageRank is at the time of this writing is a 6. (Go ahead and search for "how to do SEO." There we are, the fourth organic result on the first page, but the *New York Times* is nowhere to be seen.)[4] By balancing PageRank with its constantly changing index of the web's content, Google can provide search results that are representative of the most influential and authoritative sources even as those sources shift in either aspect. So a site with a lower PageRank, or less overall influence on the web, could have a much greater authority over a particular subject. This insight is what Chris Anderson and Clay Shirky had in mind when they popularized the idea of the long tail.[5]

It is also this differentiation that makes SEO possible. Being in control of "on page" factors—those that frame a page's content using metadata, heading specifications, friendly links—enables you to compete in the marketplace of authority.

How to Do Your Own "On Page" Optimization

Assuming you use a content management system that enables you to control the on-page factors I mentioned above, optimizing your content for search engines is actually a fairly easy process. The difficulty isn't in the implementation so much as it is in choices you make. This should become clearer as I review the various items you'll need to consider as you optimize your web pages. I'll use a page from my firm's website as an example, which you can view for yourself by going to www.newfangled.com/the_web_development_process or referring to the image on page 83.

Title Tag

The title tag, which appears at the top of your browser, is different from the title a page might display at the beginning of its content. For instance, the title of our example page (also it's H1, but more on that later) is "How a Website Is Built," which you can read right above the first paragraph. But the current title tag for this page is slightly different; it reads, "The Web Development Process." Because the title tag is one of the primary pieces of

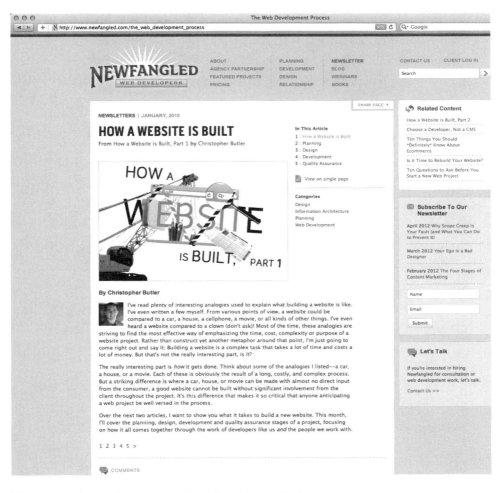

This page can be found at: www.newfangled.com/the_web_development_process.

information that Google analyzes when indexing web pages, it's important that it be an accurate description of what the page's content is actually about while also corresponding to phrases that searchers are likely to use—something our founder Eric Holter goes into much more detail about in a video on how to do SEO that is well worth your time.[6]

With that in mind, look back at the differences between the page title and the title tag for this page. The page title is probably a bit light on keywords, but I don't want it to be any longer than it needs to be (anything under seventy characters will be technically suitable for Google) because its primary purpose is to work from an editorial perspective—what is memorable and intriguing to a reader—not from a SEO perspective—what people are likely to use as a search query for information on the web development process. Search queries don't need to be grammatically correct complete sentences; they can be one word or a phrase that in combination identifies the idea you're looking for. I think this is pretty intuitive when it comes to searching—we do it every day, whether we're searching for "Google PageRank lookup," "solid state hard drive upgrade" or "cities by continuous time of habitation" (all searches I made within the last day)—but anticipating the search queries that other people might use to find your content is not so simple. You can use Google Trends (www.goog.com/trends) to evaluate search terms you're thinking of using in your title tags, but it's also probably going to take some trial and error. That's why I was careful to note above what my example page's title tag is right now. I might very well decide to tweak it at some point in the future if its performance slips.

Meta Description

Unlike the meta title, a page's meta description is not visible to users, that is, unless Google displays it on their search engine results pages (SERPs). Let me explain: The meta description is another way to identify the subject of a page's content. However, the content of the meta description will be indexed and used to populate the text of the snippet displayed when that page appears in a list of search results if it is the most relevant match for the query used. If the description is duplicate content, empty or otherwise deemed irrelevant, Google will extract content from the page itself to populate the search result snippet. The meta description for our example page is:

Building a website is a complex task that takes a lot of time and costs a lot of money. But the interesting part is how it gets done through the work of developers and their clients.

If I do a search for "the web development process," my page appears toward the top of Google's second SERP, but its snippet only displays some of my meta description:

> **Building a website is a complex task that takes a lot of time and costs a lot of money. But the interesting part is how it gets done through …**

Remember, Google controls whether a web page's meta description appears in part or at all. If it doesn't appear, there may be nothing you can do—that makes sense for your page's content, anyway—to change that. Though Google may truncate a page's description in its snippet, there is not a specific character limit to meta descriptions; you can craft something more grammatically correct than your meta title, but you still want to make sure that it contains keywords relevant to your page's subject and is as succinct as possible.

Heading Tags

The heading tags—H1 through H6—allow you to organize a page's content in a similar way as you might an outline. The H1, or largest heading, would be the title of the outline, which also means it can only appear once. Earlier I noted that the example page's title, "How a Website Is Built," is also its H1. This is because we've built our CMS to automatically display the title a user creates for a page as its H1. That ensures that there's no confusion around what the largest heading should be and, more important, that there is not more than one. As for the rest of the headings, there can be multiple of each. In fact, the page has several H2s—each of the bold headings for our calls to action in the right sidebar are wrapped in H2 tags.

Link Text and Friendly URLs

Remember how I noted that Google's PageRank algorithm was primarily concerned with the influence of a page? Well, one way that Google evaluates this is to look at the text used when linking to a page. The more descriptive it is of that page's content, the better the search engine can understand the value of its incoming links. So, if I were to link to the home page of my firm's website by writing, "click here to see our home page," I'm telling Google nothing about where I'm directing users. But if I were to link to it by writing, "Newfangled is a web development company," I'm providing Google—and readers—with a clearer idea of the nature of the content I'm linking to.

This same principle applies to the file names of web pages, which are often called "Friendly URLs." A URL that is more indicative of the database technology being used—something like, "http://www.website.com/contentmgr/showdetails.php/id/182"—doesn't do much to help Google interpret what it's about, not to mention users who need something easier to remember. If you're using an up-to-date content management system, it should include a rewrite engine that enables you to provide a Friendly URL for each of your pages.

There really is no magic to SEO. In fact, control over and thoughtful implementation of these four on-page factors—the meta title, meta description, heading tags and friendly links—is all you need to properly optimize your web content. And just so you're assured I'm not over simplifying it, they are all we use to optimize the content of our website. Of course, SEO is not a one-time procedure. It's an ongoing process. The more often you add indexable, properly optimized content to your website, the more likely you are to see significant gains in valuable traffic to your site.

So, What About Abuses of SEO?

Now that we understand how search engines work and how to optimize our content for them, we can return to those abuses I mentioned at the beginning of this article. Are there holes in this system that allow some people to take advantage of it? Sure. But none of them challenge the validity of the core principles we've learned about so far. Most are actually a matter of business ethics in general. Here's just one example:

The New York Times ran an investigative piece in 2010 focusing on an online eyeglasses retailer, DecorMyEyes, and its suspect use of SEO to build its business.[7] Author David Segal framed his story around injustice: how customer complaints can actually end up benefitting an online retailer's business because of the way search engines assess the value of incoming links. In this particular case, the volume of complaints against DecorMyEyes was shocking enough, but the way the owner participated in complaint threads—aggressively, threateningly and always encouraging the controversy—was even more so. Why would a business owner encourage and celebrate public customer complaints? Segal's article sheds some light on the mystery, concluding that DecorMyEyes is profiting by exploiting a vulnerability of Google's system: not qualitatively evaluating content. While Google representatives have not officially confirmed whether its algorithms include "sentiment analysis"—which would discern between customer complaints and commendations—the DecorMyEyes story seems to confirm that it does not. Without sentiment analysis, every new complaint customers publish online that links back to the DecorMyEyes website is web content that increases their PageRank. Even though the complaints are meant, justifiably, to damage the online influence of a shady business, they're actually doing the opposite.

But it's also not clear that sentiment analysis is the best solution to the problem. While sentiment analysis might seem helpful from a consumer's point of view, imagine how it might affect other kinds of searches. After all, public opinion isn't always rational or correct. In an interview with Segal, Danny Sullivan, editor in chief of the blog Search Engine Land, points out that you might have a hard time finding legitimate information about a politician if Google evaluated web pages on the basis of public sentiment. However, he also suggests that Google could increase the presence of consumer reviews associated with particular sites when they appear in search results. Not a bad idea, especially because it seems that only critical mass and the determination of a few of DecorMyEyes' extra-dissatisfied former customers is just now beginning to derail its long run of abuse. In the meantime, Google's intention to keep qualitative evaluation to a minimum underscores that the root of this particular problem is a flaw in people, not the system itself. No matter what system we have to work with, there will always be ways to game it.

I once wrote an article in which I concluded with the statement, "Robots don't read, people do,"[8] to remind readers that, while it's easy to become accustomed to creating search-engine-friendly content, the real point is to create content that is people friendly and then optimize it for search engines. But bearing in mind how important search engines are to our ability to navigate the web, perhaps a minor revision to that statement might be helpful: Robots don't read, but they help people who do.

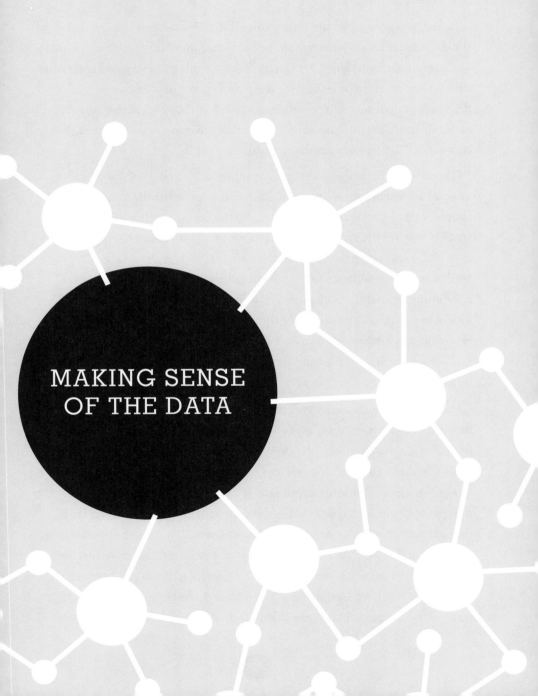

MAKING SENSE
OF THE DATA

Do you enjoy working with data?

I'm guessing your answer was a quick yes. So I'll ask again: Do you really like working with data?

Before you answer, let me clarify something. What I don't have in mind is the data visualization work we all dream about, the kind that indulges our fantasies of Tuftean[1] glory. I mean the boring stuff: gathering and analyzing data for the purpose of evaluating the performance of what we've designed—in particular, our websites. Much less flashy work, for sure, but certainly more useful. The good news is that anyone can do this kind of data work. The bad news is that few do.

Those who are realizing that perhaps they don't like working with data after all are encountering a critical barrier that prevents the long-term success of just about anything we create: the accountability of reality. The truth is that very few things are perfect on first launch; most require some evaluation and refinement before they can attain their original goals, as well as ongoing guidance to keep from falling below expectations as the conditions around them change. For websites—remember, permanent works in progress—the reality of their performance can be almost impossible to discern without access to real user data. Without the data and a commitment to measurement as a discipline, your work will likely be in vain.

Fortunately the data are easily accessible. One of the most powerful website measurement tools available today—Google Analytics—is free of charge. In the "free, but" economy of the internet, there are few free tools that don't come with some sort of catch or eventual disappointment; Google Analytics, however, is not one of them. For the time being, it is unequivocally free and packs abundant functionality that almost certainly exceeds your day-to-day needs. Convinced? Great. I'm going to be referring to it over and over again in this chapter, so if you haven't set up an account and installed it on your website, make it a priority to do so (for instance, now).Once you have Google Analytics installed and begin to accumulate traffic data, the next challenge you will face will be in determining how to use that data to evaluate the effectiveness of your website. Though a simple online search for "how to use Google Analytics" will show you that there is no shortage of free help available,[2] I'd like to first provide you a broader point of view on measurement.

Measurement Is a Way of Life

Measurement means all kinds of things to different people. In the early days of the internet, web masters, content to simply count traffic to their site, slapped visitor counters onto their home pages. The higher the number, the more the glory (and, oh, the glory when that counter advanced into the thousands!). But once database-driven websites became more common, the coveted hit—the metric everyone had come to obsess over—became irrelevant. After all, the number of times a call is made to your database, especially for graphics-heavy sites, is irrelevant to any meaningful measure of success. Eventually we got a bit more sophisticated, thanks to tools like Urchin and WebTrends, and began talking about true visits—unique website user sessions—and measuring them with enthusiasm. But even visits don't tell us much more than hits. We all know that now. The truth is that the volume of traffic a website receives is a far less relevant indicator than the action taken by the visitors that make up that traffic. This insight, the steady refining of meaningful measurement, is what led Google Analytics to sweep us all off our feet and begin our new romance with website data. By setting goals that correspond to visitor actions, we could truly see if our investment in the web was paying off. We learned that user engagement was the best measure of success.

Well, I think we all believe we've learned it. But my experience has been that, in order to tell the real story of what's going on with your website, you have to do a bit more than just track the numbers that Google Analytics—or any other tool—provides in their preconfigured reports. Measurement is a discipline, not an isolated step in the web development process. It does not happen just once; it is best made a routine. The long-term value of your website will grow as you regularly draw actionable conclusions from your measurement that help you to improve it. In order to do that, you'll ultimately need to create your own custom reports that answer the questions that only you can ask, those influenced by your unique story: why you built your website in the first place, what you hoped to achieve with it and how you've nurtured it over time as your business has changed. Remaining grounded in your ongoing story will enable you to focus your measurement, to extract meaning from metrics. Losing sight of it, on the other hand, will quickly reduce your practice to a pattern of repetitive and meaningless number watching. I'll return to the idea of creating unique reports later. But first we need to get acquainted with the language of measurement.

There are three core terms that encapsulate a corresponding series of big-picture questions that measurement should help you answer in lieu of those only-you-know-to-ask questions. These terms—*referrers*, *top content* and *bounce rate*—represent concepts with which everyone should be familiar when reviewing analytics data, especially for the first time.

The Three Big Questions

1. *Who is driving traffic to my site?* The simple answer to this question is search engines ... and everyone else. Google Analytics will help you make sense of this by breaking down your website's traffic sources, which it calls "referrers," into a tidy list ranked by visitor volume. If you've optimized your pages for search engines—specifically by paying attention to the on-page factors I outlined in chapter 6—you should be noticing an increasing volume of traffic referred from search engines. Google Analytics will also show you the most commonly used terms that led searchers to your site. Keep an eye on those. If they don't correspond with what your site is about, rework your metadata, especially your title tag. The goal here is to receive visits from the people who are looking for someone like you but don't know about you yet. As for the rest of your referrers—that long tail of unique sources comprised of everything from links you leave in blog comments to social media and press mentions—they can represent very valuable traffic in the aggregate that you'll want to nurture, as well. In fact, I'll dive a bit deeper into this in the last section of this chapter.

2. What are the most popular pages on my site? For most websites, the home page will initially receive the bulk of new visitors, keeping it at the top of Google Analytics' Top Content report. But that does not mean it will always be the first page that every visitor sees. On the contrary, many of your site's visitors will enter on a subpage of your site. Indeed, as your website's content grows, the number of entries to subpages will likely exceed those to the home page. Take a look at your site's top content and think deeply about the impression users might have after entering your site through them. While that alone is likely to cause you to rethink the information they contain, drill down a bit deeper to follow the entrance paths and see what pages users tend to navigate to next. Getting a realistic sense of flow from the user data will help you to refine the information architecture of your site.

3. How many of my site's visitors leave unsatisfied? User satisfaction is often expressed in terms of a website's bounce rate, one of the most misunderstood metrics you'll encounter in Google Analytics. Put simply, the bounce rate is the percentage of visitors who entered your site but did not continue browsing it, either because their browsing session expired or because they left your site without visiting any other pages. Consequently, conventional wisdom deems the lower the bounce rate, the better. After all, the idea is to gain and keep visitors. A high bounce rate can be the result of web pages with poorly optimized metadata, which can give search engines and their users a false sense of what they're actually about. If a user searches for one thing and lands on a page that is hardly related to her query, it makes sense that she wouldn't stick around. This is why a website's bounce rate is typically seen as an indicator of user satisfaction. However, larger sites—both in terms of content and traffic—are likely to have high bounce rates even if most users are satisfied. The more pages a website contains, the wider its topical scope is likely to be, which in turn will attract users with all kinds of needs that, while they may be addressed by individual pages, are not in line with the site's overall purpose. For example, a user may find an isolated article about web typography helpful or interesting, but that user may not explore the site that contains it any further if they're not actually looking to hire the designer who wrote it. Such a user would register as a bounce, but who's to say that she was unsatisfied? Perhaps she will return again someday, when she needs a designer, or refer someone else to the website. As we learned in chapter 3, the mind of the audience is mysterious, and not all website content should be created for a single persona. Today's influencers, though their activity may increase a website's bounce rate, are quite possibly tomorrow's decision makers. It's troubling enough that a website's bounce rate is so often qualitatively misunderstood, but sadly it is just as often quantitatively misunderstood. I'll explain how bounce rate percentages properly apply to website traffic numbers later in this chapter, in the section on Understanding Bounce Rate (page 95).

These three questions are what you might consider "Measurement 101." But what if you want to go deeper? As I mentioned earlier, the best way to do that is to gather data and assemble custom reports based upon your finely tuned and informed questioning.

Gathering Data

Google Analytics does a great job of presenting a vast array of data in many meaningful reports, but those reports can also be confusing or not quite configured to tell the particular story you're looking for. With that in mind, I'm often inclined to pull the data out of Google Analytics and into another context in order to make the connections I need to see in order to discern what's actually going on with my website's traffic. Fortunately Google Analytics offers the ability to export any report in just about any document format you might need.

I can't emphasize enough the benefit of exporting Google Analytics data. You just won't be able to make certain connections by only viewing isolated reports—particularly if you've been doing basic website measurement for a few years now and are ready to go deeper. Sometimes, in order to answer the more meaningful questions you have about your site, you'll need to create your own reports that draw from multiple analytics sources. It was by doing this that I came to an interesting conclusion about how referral traffic actually converts. In order for those conclusions to make sense, however, I need to clarify a few things about bounce rates.

Understanding Bounce Rate

Because the term *bounce rate* describes traffic that moves away from your website, it's often the metric that causes the most concern. What's worse, some get overly focused on hitting a very particular percentage without thinking about where that percentage comes from and what it applies to.

The most important principle I have learned about bounce rate is so obvious it often gets completely ignored: The bounce rate only applies to traffic that landed on a page. Unfortunately, Google Analytics makes that principle a little too easy to ignore by sequestering landing page data in one report and commonly displaying visit and bounce rate values on most others. You see, a visit is any view of any page, but a landing is a visitor's first view of any page on a website; all landings are visits, but not all visits are landings. To determine the exact number of bounces from a particular page, you must combine data from two different reports in Google Analytics—the Top Content report (or Content Detail report) and the Top Landing Pages report.

Google Analytics' Top Content and Content Detail reports list the bounce rate along with the total number of unique visits but exclude landing data, creating the false impression that the bounce rate should be applied to the total number of visits. But as we've learned, the bounce rate should only be applied to the number of visitors that landed (first entered the site) on that page—often a much lower number than the total visits, which means that the bounce rate is also likely lower than you might initially conclude. By merging data from both the Content Detail and Top Landing Pages reports, you can create a new custom report of your own that will help you to better understand the traffic to any page.

Let's explore an example to see how this works. I'm going to throw a bunch of numbers at you—real-world data, so they're not going to be tidy,

The Content Detail report in Google Analytics will tell you about the activity on an individual page of your website.

round numbers, either—as well as a bit of math, so just take it slow and stick with me.

The Content Detail report above tells me that a total of 5,863 unique visitors have come to an individual page on my site in the last month. Because this page was promoted midmonth (you can see the resulting spike of activity), I can assume that most of the visitors arrived to my website for the first time by landing on this page, but without checking the Top Landing Pages report, which will tell me the exact number, I won't know for sure. In fact, I'm likely to apply the bounce rate shown on the Content Detail report (29.19 percent, which I'll round down to an even 29 percent) to the total number of visitors, which would create the impression that 1,700 visitors bounced. That may be more than actually did bounce.

After checking out the Top Landing Pages report (page 97), I learn that 5,539 visitors landed on this page, slightly less than the total visitor number. Now, between these two reports, I want to be able to reconstruct the story of

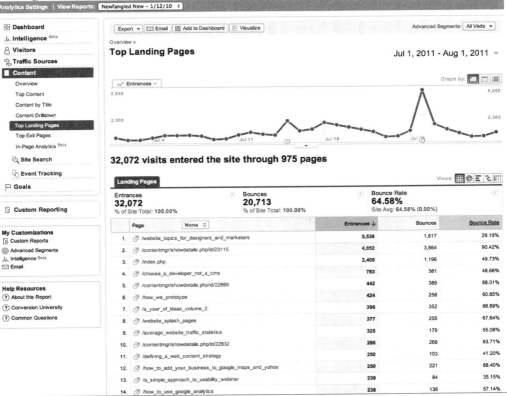

The Top Landing Pages report in Google Analytics will tell you about the pages that serve as entry points to your website for first-time visitors.

all the visitors to the page. I can do this by focusing in on the visit numbers, the bounce rate and also the percentage of visitors that exited the site after viewing this page (29.04 percent, which I'll also round down to 29 percent).

My first step is to subtract the number of visitors who landed on this page from the total number of unique views of the page—that's 5,863–5,539, which leaves me with 324. If I apply the exit percentage (29 percent) to this number, I am left with only 93—the number of visitors to this page who came to it from another page on our website but then decided to leave. This is different from the bounce rate, which, as I mentioned before, identifies the portion of landing traffic that left the site without viewing any other pages. To determine the number of bounces, I apply the bounce rate

(29 percent) to the number of users who landed on this page (5,539), which gives me 1,606 bounces. This is less than I thought before investigating the landing traffic data.

By doing this bit of math, I now know that out of the total 5,863 visitors to this page, 5,539 entered my site for the first time on it (landed), 1,606 left right away (bounced), 93 left our site from this page after having viewed other pages (exited) and 4,164 continued from it on to other pages. Now 1,606 is only 23 percent of the total traffic to this page, leaving 4,257 others that at least saw some additional content on my site—that's 73 percent of its total traffic.

As you can see, separating the data and doing a little bit of work to get the numbers right is worthwhile. If I hadn't done this, I probably would have assumed that a 29 percent bounce rate (granted, a very low rate) for my web page meant that 1,700 of its visitors bounced, when in reality, 1,606 of them did. That may seem like an insignificant difference, but consider this: The difference is not just a number, it is 94 more people than the Content Detail report made it seem. In human terms, discovering an additional 94 people that were exposed to your message is very significant!

What Does This Mean for Conversions?

If I apply a custom segment to these reports, I can get an even more detailed view of the story of the visitors to my page. Creating a custom segment that adds in conversion data to my reports will enable me to see which visitors to this (or any other) page ended up completing a goal—say, filling out a contact form, registering for an event or subscribing to my newsletter.

Suppose that 2,900 visitors of this page (49%) also completed goals and that the Top Landing pages report tells me that 2,750 of these were completed by visitors who landed on this page. That leaves the remaining goals (150) completed by those non-landing visitors (324). If I parse these two amounts, I can conclude that 95% of landing traffic to this page converted, while only 46% of visitors that viewed this page among others during their session converted. Because this page is a landing page for our website's newsletter, it makes sense that landing traffic would be compelled to sign up for our newsletter (the main conversion point available on this page). These numbers show me quite clearly that the page is doing exactly what it was designed to do.

The Value of Referrals

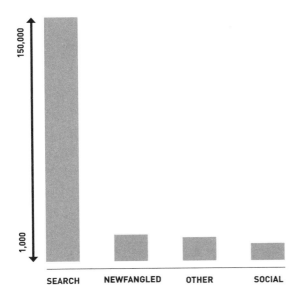

**TOP 4 REFERRERS
BY CATEGORY**
2010 - 2011

Looking at what visitors do once they've arrived at your site—exactly what we just did in the preceding example—will tell you a lot about how your content enables certain user behavior, particularly conversions. But that's only one piece of the puzzle. To understand even more about why some visitors convert, we need to look at where they came from.

In the graph above, I've grouped and plotted the top four referrers to my firm's website (www.newfangled.com) over the past year as an example. To assemble this data, I first needed to extract a much longer list of about one hundred unique referrers from Google Analytics, the number of visits each referred to my website and the number of those visitors that converted by engaging with one of the website's several calls to action. Once I had the full list, I grouped each entry into one of four categories: *Search*, which included all the major search engines; *Social*, which included any website that could be considered a social network (i.e., Facebook, Twitter, LinkedIn, and Google+); *Newfangled*, which included our own newsletter and blog digest email campaigns; and *Other*, which included a very long tail of unique websites that linked to Newfangled. As the graph makes quite plain, organic search generated far more traffic to Newfangled.com than any other category of referral sources.[3] But in making that fact clear, the graph obscures the really interesting story the data tell.

The problem with this kind of visualization is obvious: Because the top contributing category (Search) brings more than ten times the traffic than the next most active referrer (Newfangled), the graph portrays three out of the four categories as contributing relatively the same amount of traffic. Consequently, it could be simplified down to Search vs. everything else. But that isn't a very helpful story, especially in light of the fact that despite bringing huge numbers of traffic to our site, the Search category performs dismally when it comes to conversions.

The Familiarity Spectrum

Here's where things get interesting. For a site like Newfangled.com, which receives such a large volume of referral traffic from search engines, simply plotting out the top referral sources is pretty much a waste of time. With thousands of pages drawing in thousands of visitors with all kinds of interests, only a very small subset of those visits are likely to be interested in making contact with a web development company. So, it's no surprise that the percentage of visitors referred by search engines that convert would be low compared to other sources. The principle makes perfect sense when you think about it—and remember, we're talking about organic search engine traffic here, not pay-per-click listings—people trust people, and people act upon trust.

But I think there's an important nuance to that principle that's worth considering. When I plot out the top referrers to my firm's site, the general point still stands: Organic search traffic accounts for the largest portion of incoming traffic, but a comparatively small amount of it converts (1 percent), while Social brings far fewer visitors but performs better in terms of conversions (2 percent). But the astounding thing is the traffic referred from those sites that fall in the Other category, a very long list that spans an equally broad spectrum of activity, produced significantly more engagement. A few sites refer very large numbers of visitors, but most refer less than one hundred over the course of the year One particular website, *Smashing Magazine* (www.SmashingMagazine.com) was the dominant single driver of traffic, referring thousands of visitors on its own, 74 percent of which converted in some way. But our own email campaigns, which offer conversion opportunities by linking to upcoming webinars or being forwarded to nonsubscribers, fall below the Other category when it comes to conversions (8 percent). In the grand scheme of things, its performance is still great; I consider anything above 1 percent as decent. But, it is diminished by the performance of the traffic referred by *Smashing Magazine* despite targeting an audience that is far more familiar with us and what we do than *Smashing Magazine*'s diverse audience of hundreds of thousands of readers. Why is this? Here's where the familiarity spectrum comes in.

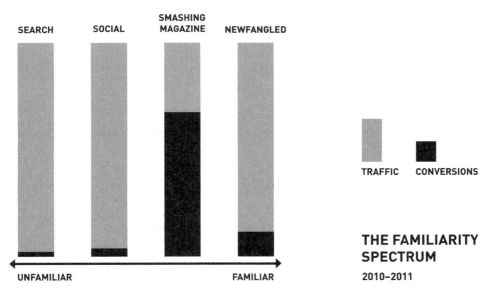

At the top of the familiarity spectrum are those referrers that are the most unfamiliar with their own audience, like search engines. Search engines are robots, and though they're used by millions to find information every day, their "recommendations" drop in value compared to those that users receive from other human beings. Social networks, on the other hand, are websites shaped by their users—where proximity in connection tends to increase familiarity. Between Twitter, Facebook and LinkedIn, Newfangled has several thousand connections, which extends our reach considerably. By sharing information and soliciting feedback over these networks, the familiarity anyone within them will have with my firm will obviously be greater than a searcher referred to us by a search engine, but in many cases, the "connection" is still, for all intents and purposes, a stranger, which places this category next in the spectrum. *Smashing Magazine*, on the other hand, has a different kind of connection with its readers, one strengthened by brand loyalty. Like any popular publication, *Smashing*'s readers trust them to give valuable information and recommendations and are likely to act in response. This is evident from the participation level of the readers on *Smashing*'s own site and from the value of the traffic we've received from them—the familiarity here is what keeps the magazine afloat. Thus, *Smashing Magazine* represents the "Other" category next on the spectrum. But at the most familiar end of the spectrum is our own subscriber base, a group of people who are as engaged with us as anyone could be without being a client or employee. They've already converted in the past—when they signed up to receive our emails—and it's going to take a bit more for them to convert again. Think about it this way: Given the choice of professional recommendations from a robot, a stranger, the President or your grandmother, which one are you likely to act upon? Sometimes closeness doesn't equal priority!

What to Do?

As these visualizations demonstrate, referral traffic is one of the most important sources of data that you have available within the analytics environment. Beyond the inclination to be gratified when someone else links to you, studying referral traffic will yield a deep understanding of the rich ecosystem in which your website exists. Look at your own referrers. You've probably got some robot-referred activity (Search), some less-than-familiar social network stuff (Twitter, Facebook, LinkedIn) and probably even some from your own marketing initiatives, like email campaigns. But what about more influential recommendations? You may not be able to get a nod from the President, but I'm sure there are influencers within your network that would love to point people your way. If you haven't done so already, seek them out. Don't ask for a link (that's so 1998), but build a relationship with them so that the referral is implicit in all kinds of activity between you, whether that be within social networks, participation in blog conversations or something else. You may even be able to deepen that relationship by writing articles or creating other content for them on their turf. But don't expect to reconvert the already converted—those who already subscribe to your content or have engaged with you in some other way. Focus your efforts on spreading new seed in the most fertile ground you can find. The "sweet spot" of the familiarity spectrum is going to be just shy of the most familiar audience you have, probably among those connected strongly to an influencer with whom you could build a strong, mutually beneficial relationship. By looking closely at your conversion data and using the techniques I have described in this chapter, you should be able to pinpoint whom that might be.

CONTENT

Everyone is talking about content. Googling the phrase *content strategy* (a query more specific to my line of work) retrieves over 100 million results[1]—a clear indicator that interest in content is very much in the zeitgeist. By the time you read this, I expect that number will have grown even higher. But I also suspect that the substance of the talk would be quite different if content were truly respected. I believe this because the way we talk about content is beginning to sound a lot like the way we talk about money.

The trouble with that is we don't really get money, either. Few are foolish enough to say it aloud, but the actions of many betray a single fallacy that remains the pernicious root of recurring fiscal irresponsibility: that with enough money, any problem can be solved. Removed from crisis, safely reading this book, we know this to be untrue. We've seen it. We've lived through it. Yet, we continue to obsess over how much we have and how much more we think we need. Money, however, is not simply a quantitative measure of units—a figure that can be repeatedly plugged into an equation until it produces something positive. Money is a representation of value. It is a symbol—not a quantitative measure, but a qualitative one. Indeed, the concept of value is a chimera; it evades objective meaning just as readily from one person to another as it does for the same person from one context to another. Consider movie tickets: Breaking down a $10 ticket to its cost per minute—roughly 11 cents for a two-hour picture—gets you no closer to a true valuation of the movie as would assuming its initial production costs are a relevant indicator. After all, could anyone seriously argue that the phenomenally bad *2012*'s $200 million price tag made it a better film than *The King's Speech*, an Academy Award-winning independent production that cost only $15 million? Neither the length of a movie, nor how much it cost to make, can predict value, at least as far as the consumer is concerned. But after the last frame fades from view, ask any moviegoer about value and you'll certainly get strong responses. The duration alone doesn't satisfy. It will be on the subjective basis of quality whether seeing a film is worth $10. That much is plain to viewers yet elusive to creators who have other pressures formulating their expectations of success. As this simple example shows, when it comes to money, we could certainly stand to distance ourselves from a units-based perspective and consider the story that a qualitative perspective tells.

One day, I imagine, it will be clear that our insistence upon focusing only on the quantitative was at least in part responsible for how we ended up in such a mess back in 2008. We may wish for a formula to solve our financial woes, but I believe we know that they are rooted in our system of value, not in our system of measure.

Sadly, the same thing is happening in marketing. Whereas a disconnect between money and value has created disastrous fiscal bubbles, a disconnect between content and value is inflating a bubble of its own. Content—today's currency of attention—has taken the place of money as the panacea that will solve all problems. To be sure, vanity is also a factor here. The visibility an individual or group can have today as a result of content is unprecedented, motivating production when perhaps silence might be wiser. But, I am more interested here in exploring the inflation of content's business value than the inflation of egos. After the last recession, we now know enough about bubbles to be able to watch this one inflate from the inside. As I write this, I'm overwhelmed by content—everything from blogs to books—by marketers, social scientists and others, who are studying in detail the expanding content bubble from their unique points of view, fascinated by the transformative force of creativity on society, especially of course on marketing, but perhaps discounting the fact that they write from within it. The complexity of content surely merits study, but my simple understanding of what is happening is this: Because we can create content, we do.

In the first chapter of this book, I asked the question, "What is the web?" and took the "scenic route" to the answer, however subjective it may be. But I suppose a more accessible definition could be that the web simply is content. In an article written for *SEED* magazine about our struggle to manage the information we've produced (among other things), Iris Vargas accounted for the almost incomprehensibly large corpus of digital content in the world.[2] She wrote:

As of January 2010, the total amount of digital content that humans had collectively produced was estimated at 1 zettabyte. To put this into perspective, the letter "z" in a standard Word document amounts to roughly 1 byte. A typed page comes to about 2,000 bytes. A high-resolution photograph? 2 million bytes, or megabytes. Add six more zeros and you get two terabytes—the equivalent of all the information contained in the U.S. academic research library. Another six zeros (we're now at 18) brings us to the exabyte. Five exabytes, according to some scholars, could store all the words ever spoken by human beings. One thousand exabytes equals one zettabyte, the total amount of digital content in the world as of this time last year.

One zettabyte sure does sound impressive, but its meaning is still elusive. We easily understand megabytes and gigabytes—even terabytes—and can visualize the space they require by thinking of the portable hard drives we carry around. But envisioning a zettabye? I'm not sure I can do that in the same way. That's where Eli Pariser comes in. In his fascinating book, *The Filter Bubble*,[3] he offers a bit more detail on the specific kinds of content that account for these numbers:

We are overwhelmed by a torrent of information: 900,000 blog posts, 50 million tweets, more than 60 million Facebook status updates, and 210 billion e-mails are sent off into the electronic ether every day. Eric Schmidt likes to point out that if you recorded all human communication from the dawn of time to 2003, it'd take up about 5 billion gigabytes of storage space. Now we're creating that much data every two days.

Accounting for the kinds of content that make up this massively growing corpus is helpful—I know what a typical blog post looks like. Granted, much of the content that Vargas and Pariser mention (e.g., status updates, emails and the like) is not typically what we'd consider web content, but enough of it is to infer a sobering point: The web does not need any more content.

And yet, content is the point of every website. For those who design things for the web, this provides a bit of a paradox, doesn't it? Amidst a glut of content, one is left to question, *What is it all for?*

Our collective prolificacy makes at least one thing quite clear: We value content. Or, at least we think we do. Gaining insight into value, its subjectivity notwithstanding, has always been the pursuit of advertising. And today, the assumption of the value of content—undifferentiated as it is—has been enough to create a new "currency" in marketing (or employing a historical metaphor more fitting of the frenzy let loose by Web 2.0, a new Gold Rush). In scrambling to get a piece of the action, we build our marketing strategies upon the same logic of *more* that failed to keep financial collapse at bay: If we create enough content, people will pay attention to us and line up, ready to buy.

But content isn't free; even lousy content costs something. And if a balance sheet doesn't include a budget line for content creation, it's not detailed enough. Someone is paying for it, in time.

In this regard, content marketing has taken many of its cues from the wrong source: print publishing. The publishing industry—magazines, especially—has been propped up by advertising, which is problematic on two levels. The first is that advertising-subsidized publishing avoids the reality of the true cost of content. Before it even reaches the reader, the value of content is distorted. Without some advertising, readers would have to pay the full cost—something that publishers at some point believed would be impossible, thus creating a self-fulfilling prophecy. This leads to the second problem—that a system that has always depended upon subsidies will tend to carve a path of least resistance. Rather than slowly weaning off advertising and increasing the cost to the reader, it will instead depend more heavily upon advertising and reduce the cost to the reader.

That is, until the ratio reaches an imbalance and readers begin to question why they are paying to see ads. This is a simple law of, well, economics. Before the bubble pops, readers will accept that advertisers have a subtle, unspoken editorial control. But as soon as a tipping point is reached where advertising volume supersedes everything else, readership will begin to drop for one simple reason: Their sense of value has been violated.

In 2008, when the overall market experienced a significant decline, magazine advertising dropped by almost 12 percent. That may not sound like much, but when you consider that only forty-two magazines saw an increase in advertising of any kind that year, the dramatic reality of the situation becomes clearer. In fact, *Folio Magazine* pointed out that it was the "biggest dropoff since 2000, the earliest year comparative PIB numbers are available."[4] I personally remember receiving a much slighter than usual issue of *Advertising Age* in 2009 and chuckling at a sticker placed over the masthead that read, "Marketing in a Recession: It might be only 28 pages, but it's jam-packed with good advice."[5] Though I was aware that the previous issues' bulk was inflated by ads, not by more content, picking up the newly lean and austere twenty-five-page issue certainly made me question my subscription. Advertising, it seems, has not only played an integral role in the economics of publishing, it has also created an illusion of health. I had to see *AdAge* reduced to almost nothing in order to realize that, for me, the value hadn't been there for quite some time.

Unfortunately, the imbalance between advertising and content intrinsic to the print publishing industry has not substantially changed in its online form. In fact, it's gotten worse. Just about every mass media website has an immediately obvious imbalance of ads and content. Take a moment to open an article from your favorite site—you know, *The Huffington Post*, I Can Has Cheezburger, Perez Hilton or *Engadget*, for example (these, for better or for worse, are the most popular sites on the web today)—and notice how the page is filled mostly with peripheral stuff that has very little to do with the article on the page. "Stuff," by the way, isn't meant to be casual; it should be the new standard term for content that is carelessly stuffed into every last pixel available to it. After all, when I use the word *content*, advertisements, social media widgets and lures to even more (supposedly related) content aren't what I have in mind at all. Nonetheless, by force of volume, stuff is evidently what the publishers value more than content. Surveying pages like these, you certainly shouldn't conclude that enabling users to read is high up on the priority list for online publishers, either. Nor are many other things that readers—or designers, for that matter—hold sacred.

If publishers don't care whether their websites' content is read, what do they care about? It's simple; they care about clicks, because clicks validate advertising. Mass media publishers know that their websites receive such a high volume of traffic that crowding their pages with as many opportunities for users to click makes statistical sense. When hundreds of thousands of users access a web page on a daily basis, it's highly probable that a significant number of them will click a link (any link will do) that either continues their visit or sends them elsewhere via a paid advertisement. Either scenario is valuable to the publisher. A click on an ad, well that's just easy money; a click to another page on the site just increases the chance that the visitor will eventually click an ad. At this level, it simply doesn't matter if the visitor's experience with content is satisfying. For publishers, it is about volume; that's all. The more visitors their websites get, the more money they make. This is shock and awe; the special ops go on behind the scenes, and there's no hero stuff going on. It's number crunching and content farming all the way up.

It may sound cynical, but quality couldn't factor any less in most mass media content strategy. This isn't just true on the web. The statistical value of volume is at the heart of cable television programming, as well. Cable news, especially, employs the same shotgun tactics of the website publishers I've been describing, except instead of measuring the value of viewer attention in terms of page views and clicks, they measure it by the amount of time viewers remain dialed in to their broadcast. By creating the illusion that important news is happening all the time—so much so that a perpetual feed of news runs at the base of most programs while the rest of the screen is divided, Brady Bunch style, into smaller boxes of talking heads, social media commentary and, of course, sponsored messages—cable news captures us in a steady yet unsatisfying trance and leads us on with repeated promises that the really important stuff is "coming up, just after this." Television has the added advantage of being able to speak, literally, to both viewers and listeners, simultaneously weaving complex and unrelated audio and visual messages in and out of its programming, while our brains filter out only the information that is relevant to us. Unfortunately for readers' attention, that just doesn't work well on the web.

Yet, the advertising-subsidized publishing model carried over from print to the web has worked as well as those that profit from it require. In fact, it has worked so well that advertisement-subsidized content has reached an inflection point at which the better phrase is content-subsidized advertising. But the term you're likely more familiar with is one I used earlier: *content farming*, the process of creating content with such great prolificacy—if not promiscuity—that it becomes purely a platform for advertising. Put simply, a content farm is distinguished by its prioritization of advertising opportunity over quality of content—a disingenuousness made clear to any user who arrives at one from a search only to find its articles too brief, too promotional or just too stupid to be useful. Just as there is no such thing as unlawful stupidity, there are, of course, no regulations against stupidity online. Adam Gopnik, commenting in the *New Yorker* on the "cognitive exasperation" of the online experience, put it in terms I immediately connected with when he wrote, "Our trouble is not the over-all absence of smartness but the intractable power of pure stupidity, and no machine, or mind, seems extended enough to cure that."[6] Nevertheless, Google will try—the irony of its effort notwithstanding. Though the minds behind Google have taken a clear stand against content farming—and implicitly, for the machine arbitration of quality—by updating their algorithm to pinpoint its harvest,[7] content farming is actually a logical extrusion of what Google created in the first place.

This entire system—the complex interweaving of consumer demand for content and various industries' demand for consumer attention—as far as it exists online, has been perpetuated by search engines. Because search engines are best suited to index words, written content has become the focus of marketing. You've no doubt heard the very popular marketing motto that epitomizes this: "Content is King." I, for one, couldn't think of a worse catchphrase. Forgiving the sense of entitlement engendered by the word *king*, shouldn't a phrase like this be aspirational instead, linking content and value in a way that causes us to reach for something bigger than us, better and more true, rather than complacently accepting a slave economy in which we almost certainly exist at the bottom? While there is nothing inherently wrong with profitably matching user interest with content—specifically, in the various ways in which Google does so—the absence of value as an essential and reliable factor in the equation, as well as the fact that the structure of this economy is strongest when content is text, makes for the instability we are experiencing. Indeed, it has lead me to question numerous times, for myself and my clients, whether written content is truly the best way to represent expertise.

There are, in fact, plenty of instances in which the written content model is undeniably inadequate. With a few exceptions, most consumer products are not easily marketed with much text. Typically, consumers prefer to let products "speak for themselves" both in use and in researches of their performance in reviews—which, of course, are found in abundant supply on the web—rather than defer to what the maker has to say about his wares. In most cases, our aversion to being sold is so strong that it leads us to struggle to believe the seller even when we believe in the value of his product! Those in the health-care industry may also perceive reasons to take up content strategies of their own, but often locality and emergency are the primary factors in a consumer's choice of care providers, rather than researched, advance consideration. Similarly, utility-type services— plumbers, electricians, mechanics, and cleaners—are more likely to be selected on the basis of what is nearby, immediately available and affordable than any pitch a blog or newsletter may provide. That isn't to say that some form of content shouldn't occupy a piece of the overall marketing strategy; there may be opportunities to use audio, video and social media that could be quite effective, while not being the lead marketing initiative.

On the other hand, there are instances in which written content marketing works quite well. At the product end of the business spectrum, those manufactured for businesses (rather than consumers), are typically heavily researched by buyers—who make active use of search engines to do so—before purchase. Case studies, whitepapers, blog posts and other articles can satisfy the researcher's need for sharable, decision-reinforcing information, especially if they are enabling a buying decision that will ultimately be made by someone else. The same dynamic exists within any "knowledge industry" service. For professionals in design, advertising, marketing, public relations, law or finance, the essential intangibility of their expertise must be carefully described in depth in diverse ways to qualify the specific nature of what they do and for whom they are best suited to do it.

I list these considerations in order to point out that our role as strategic advisors to our clients is not to promulgate the latest marketing practices but to diagnose their needs and prescribe the best solution. Content marketing, though essential to the success of some enterprises, will not be the best fit for others. Naturally, our own fraught experience in employing content marketing for ourselves may be instructive of that point as well.

To many designers, marketers and other advertising professionals, content marketing presents many challenges, the most dire of which is so rarely discussed that most don't realize it exists until they've struggled (if not failed) with creating content for so long that they're ready to give up for good. The problem is that, when all is said and done—when we've accepted that writing content and optimizing it for search engines is critical to expressing expertise on the web in a way that increases qualified, likely-to-convert traffic to your website[8]—many of us never wanted to be writers in the first place. Not every expert wants to write. Yet somehow, we've found ourselves facing the prospect of spending more and more of our time creating content that describes what we do than doing that actual thing we do best, whether that be design or something else. It is this conflict, in concert with other factors—those I've explored so far in this chapter having to do with the glut and occasional misappropriation of content, as well as the limited mental bandwidth we each have to filter useful signal out of the noise—that often predetermines a parabolic trajectory to many a content marketing plan. What begins with a burst of enthusiasm and creativity rises to an early peak only to plummet just as fast as it began in rapid stages, from exhaustion to frustration, hopelessness, then bitterness. In the end, in the dysphoric coda, one questions everything: *I'm a designer. Why am I doing this?* If you have asked this question, whether in a similar struggle or something a bit less dramatic, you are not alone. While some have discovered an affinity for writing and gladly add it to their repertoire, many once-confident designers contend greatly with it, the strain coloring the rest of their professional practice and reducing them to a feeling of inadequacy that only builds with the decline of their energy.

The rise and fall of the content marketer will almost certainly lead to a redefinition of the role of content within marketing, as well as a redistribution of labor that more closely corresponds with the reality that not everyone is a writer, just as not everyone is a designer. Search engines, which provided the inception of this new writing industry, will also likely provide a needed transition to something more sustainable. As the technology today is best optimized to interpret meaning and expertise from indexable text, the technology of tomorrow will be capable of doing the same thing with content in less tangible forms. Authority algorithms will process sound, video, social media and any other data relevant to discerning expertise—tenure, revenue, growth, recommendations, professional certifications—in addition to text, reducing the inordinate pressure placed today on individuals to make what was once a peripheral discipline in their profession a central one.

In the meantime, creating content remains a challenge we must address practically. If you don't want to do something, you're likely to either struggle with doing it at all or with doing it consistently and effectively. As I have already explored, the desire to create marketing material is not present within everyone, which presents a dilemma to content marketers working today: Those who should do it are often least likely to do it well.

A solution to this predicament is unlikely to present itself spontaneously, nor is any content strategy alone airtight enough to prevent creators from struggling. The key is in understanding the different roles necessary to fulfill a content strategy in a sustainable way. In her excellent book, *The Elements of Content Strategy*, Erin Kissane stresses the importance of discerning between those who conceive of the strategy and those who create the content as a means of preserving quality and output over time:[9]

> In its purest form, content strategy does not produce content. It produces plans, guidelines, schedules, and goals for content, but not the substance itself, except inasmuch as examples are required to illustrate strategic recommendations. But if you have the ability to create good content, you'll have a real advantage over content strategists who do not.

This is a significant distinguishing factor that is often overlooked. In fact, while many of the firms I have consulted have enthusiastically adopted the content-marketing approach to their website and quickly conceived of a feasible content strategy, just as many have failed to maintain a consistent implementation of it. This is largely due to a lack of leadership. A successful content strategy relies less upon the content itself—though that is certainly an essential element—than it does upon a person who is able to inspire those who create the content, coalescing their unique voices around a consistent point of view, even as the stream of conversation around them ebbs and flows. Depending upon the size of the team, this person may or may not create content themselves; a truly hard line between roles may not be necessary unless the content output is great enough to merit it. In my firm, for example, I perform this role, among others, while also producing plenty of content of my own. The more important facet of this role is the authority and responsibility that accompanies it. This person, regardless of the title he or she may carry, must consider the direction of the firm's content marketing a major part of his or her job description. Though I came down hard upon the print publishing industry for the ways their economic foundations devalue content, their editors in chief—whose production, if any, is secondary to their leadership—provide the best example of how this role should function.

For those who create content, of course, the content itself is a priority. But no single piece of content, no matter how excellent, will be as successful as a steady, long-term flow of quality content. This is why the success of any content marketing strategy is achieved by committed leadership. While the leader's job is first and foremost to ensure that the point of view remains consistent with the firm's purpose and that quality is preserved, various management techniques will also be critical to sustaining the production of fresh material. Ways of dealing with the complexity of content marketing will vary greatly by the size of the organization, but two particular techniques, establishing a work flow—the process by which content is conceived, executed, evaluated, approved and delivered—and establishing an editorial calendar—which identifies topics, content types, authors and deadlines in advance—are essential to teams of all sizes. The various points of the work flow process, especially those that place quality control barriers between the content creators and the websites on which their content will eventually be found, are those which require the team to be role diversified. Kristina Halvorson's book, *Content Strategy for the Web*,[10] is a comprehensive enough treatment of the topic to serve as the primary handbook for anyone involved in content marketing, whether leading, managing or producing.

Though strengthened by proactive, intentional leadership and management, your content marketing strategy will still be vulnerable to struggling with something mysterious enough to slip through the cracks of any well-conceived machine: the creative process of producing the content itself. Writing, especially, is difficult to do well and often. As I explored earlier, it requires a level of focus and investment that can sometimes come into direct conflict with the job you'd rather do, whether that is design or something else. One solution may be to employ dedicated writers, but few marketing teams have that luxury. The reality is that, for now, many designers will have to write and create other forms of content in order to sustain their livelihoods. It is not within the scope of this book to offer advice on how to write well—there are many fine resources on that topic[11]—but I can share some insight by invoking what I call the nonwritten disciplines of writing.

There are four nonwritten disciplines that make for successful professional writing: reading, planning, research and editing. None can be left out; each is just as important as the other. But, if I had to choose one to prioritize, it would be reading. Reading is a discipline that many books on writing strangely leave out. (The other three—planning, research and editing—are all essential pieces of the content work flow that are covered in great detail by many of the excellent content marketing books I have referenced in the notes for this chapter.) Yet, there is no writing without reading. Or, maybe better said, there is no *good* writing without reading. If you want to write, or need to write—the two need not be in agreement—you must make reading a part of your life. (If you are thinking to yourself, *I don't like to read*, I'm going to promise you right now that's not true; you just have yet to find what you like.) Any aspiring writer, for whatever purpose, must actively seek out writing, in any form, that covers the topics they're interested in, even if those are not the topics they need to cover in their writing. Reading is about exposing yourself to new ideas so that your thinking—which need not be truly novel to merit writing about—can be enriched by the insights of others. There is an art to revealing ideas through the written word, one which good writers practice primarily with restraint, reserving the majority of their knowledge as an unwritten foundation for what they actually put to words— the tip of the iceberg.[12] As reading will supply much of the knowledge that makes up the background of your writing, it is indispensable.

I began this chapter by looking at the staggering volume of content available on the web and challenging our sense of its value and purpose. When content is seen purely as a means to an end, as a unit as divorced from value as our currency so often is, it will tend toward an articulation that is so cheap as to have no hope of achieving even its ill-conceived goals. On the other hand, when content is not focused enough upon a concrete goal—even one that may not be particularly motivating to a writer, like advertising—it can just as easily head in the opposite direction, self-indulgently alienated from its purpose and with no other future than online obscurity. It's not that nobody reads purposeless content (very few do, though), but nobody takes action after reading it. Eliciting action, whether that be buying a product, service or even just an idea, is a worthy purpose for any piece of content—and one that should shape how it is conceived, produced and promoted.

Promotion, of course, presents plenty of difficulties of its own, far too many to cover adequately in this book. This entire chapter, from the admonition to restore content to its own gold standard to the process by which the purpose of content should align with the purpose of the business, could be reframed to address the content we create to promote our content. Indeed, our email blasts, comments on forums, message boards or other blogs, as well as our social media engagement, is all, in the end, content. Yet, it has a slightly different purpose. Any of these kinds of promotion, insofar as they are done to increase awareness of your content, share that goal of eliciting action. But in this case, the action is not "buying" anything but simply agreeing to offer attention toward what you have to say. The job of promotion should be to enable your content to do its job. When the relationship between content and promotional content is reversed—when it's all promotion—ugly things happen. It certainly doesn't take much time for an intelligent person to perceive when the emperor has no clothes, or for that person to spread the word far and wide. In that regard, it bears considering that what we say to get attention is very different from what we say once we have it.

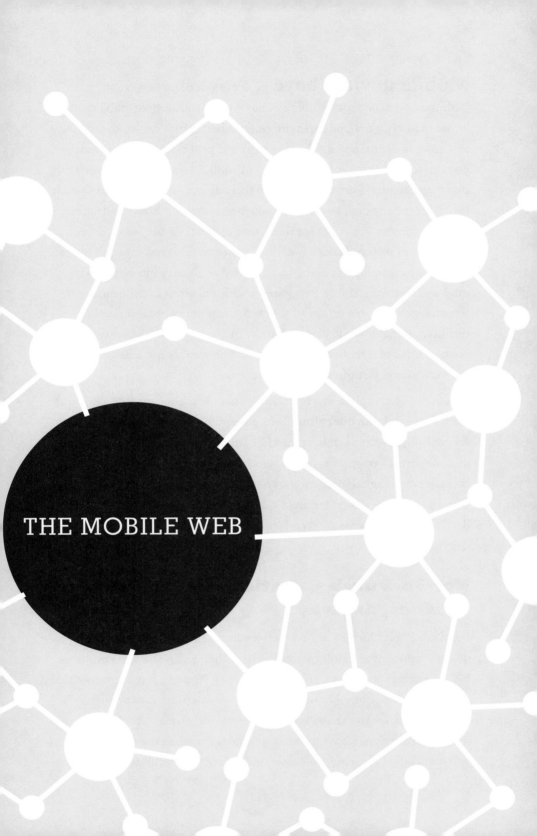

THE MOBILE WEB

Mobile devices have proliferated to such an extent that with their virtually instant ubiquity has come an illusion of stability of the entire industry surrounding them. But it is better that we see the industry as a laboratory: despite its initial success and profitability, not yet reliable enough to establish a robust "theory" of mobile strategy upon which our planning can rest assured. We are still figuring out so many things in such rapidly revolving cycles—how to make better devices, how to adapt content for them, repeat—that neither the device makers nor the content creators can afford to stop and take a breath. The situation is challenging but not futile; I am certainly not going to advocate we all bury our heads in the sand and wait for stability. Being very much a believer in the immediately leverage-able, flexible power of the web, the point of view on mobile technology that I would like to share with you is unblushingly web and content focused. Hence the title: "the mobile web" is not a new thing; it is the same thing, just through a new screen.

I am going to explore in a bit more detail how mobile devices work and the role they play in our culture before weighing the pros and cons of app and web-focused approaches to mobile strategy. But first, I am happy to offer my overall opinion as it stands today in short: Those employing a content-based digital marketing strategy should continue to focus on the web and adaptive design for mobile devices rather than dilute their focus by developing for the apps marketplaces. I will spend the rest of this chapter defending this statement …

Not-So-Dumb Question: What Are Mobile Devices, Anyway?

I think it doesn't hurt to begin by reviewing the basics—what mobile devices represent technologically and how their use is shaping culture— before getting into any specifics about mobile strategy. It is important that we not take for granted how significant their invention is as an industrial milestone, so, forgive me as I restate the obvious: Today's mobile device (I'm generally thinking of the smartphone rather than the tablet, though I will use a tablet in an example later) is the first successful synthesis of three distinct types of devices that have been well integrated into our culture for some time now—devices that enable communication, entertainment and productivity. The most innovative and successful smartphones—clearly pioneered by the iPhone—collapse the telephone, television, stereo, book and personal computer all into one pocket-sized object that, in large part because of its unprecedented portability, has become one of our most desired, valued and trusted possessions. Each of these previously distinct devices once received our undivided attention, yet today, must share it with the others. That is why thinking of mobile devices as trifocal is critical to understanding them: How we engage with a device and content—and the degree to which our attention is focused on either—has everything to do with whether a device and the content created for it is effective. Remember, these devices are not just fancy phones, nor are they just tiny computers. They are something new—a fusion that is still taking shape and shaping the world around it.

Because of this new synthesis of communication + entertainment + productivity, mobile devices are naturally having a profound effect on content. Phone calls, text messages, photos, videos, blogs, tweets, TV shows, movies, podcasts, music and much more are all being transmitted to and through the same object. By funneling content previously crafted for three discreet devices through one, the content experience is consolidated—blurring the cognitive edges between communication, entertainment and productivity. That alone is having a huge impact on how we think about content—how it's created, designed, delivered, consumed and shared.[1] But, this consolidation is also exposing the fractured nature of the content experience: Some content is designed to adapt, reshaping to fit a variety of contexts from desktop to tablet to smartphone, while other content is not. One website is usable, another is not. One video plays, another doesn't. You get the idea; you've experienced it for yourself.

Rather than take a wait-and-see approach, hoping that the fractured content experience will resolve itself eventually (it won't; nothing does), we should see this transition for the opportunity it truly is. Every glitch, hiccup or disappointment elicits raw, actionable feedback. When we find the mobile web experience wanting, we immediately think, *It should work this way, instead.* In other words, we solve the problem in our minds. But we don't stop there. Being in the midst of the mobile experience, we don't just know how to better optimize content for smaller, portable conditions, we go further, reimagining it as something far more flexible than it was before. Mobile devices are nothing short of a game changer for the entire content experience. We should be taking notes now, while everything is still messy.

On that note, allow me just a brief digression ...

Understanding Mobile by the Numbers

While there is no shortage of awestruck reporting of the numbers associated with mobile—you've read the blog posts, the tweets and the PowerPoints (oh, God, the PowerPoints)—I think a brief review of them is still in order. Tomi Ahonen notes that there are currently 5.2 billion active mobile subscribers, or in other words, 75 percent of the world's population.[2] Take a moment to let that sink in.

It is important that we first parse out how many of those 5.2 billion mobile subscribers actually use a smartphone and access the web with it. That number is far less: 975 million, again, according to Ahonen's *Almanac 2011*. (You should really open that and save it for later, as it is full of details worth knowing.) Still, 975 million is a very large number, and it is expected to continue growing at an extremely fast rate. Drilling down even more, 625 million mobile subscribers access the web using only a mobile device. That statistic, though perhaps difficult to imagine, is true and should reframe how you think about your own website and whether it needs to adapt for mobile access.

Ahonen also provides some statistics that should help measure our enthusiasm about app development—something I will also challenge shortly for other reasons. Contrary to popular assumptions, the majority of app revenues so far has actually been produced by proprietary enterprise-level applications—the type of thing that syncs up large companies' fleets of Blackberries to their e-mail and other internal systems—not the fun, shiny apps we think about in the Apple and Android marketplaces. Those apps represented a total of $3 billion in revenue in 2010, which, for perspective, was only 1 percent of the year's total revenues produced by mobile data activity. Text messaging completely eclipsed that, representing somewhere in the neighborhood of $120 billion.

These statistics tell a nuanced story that is often glossed over in the effusive hand waving that goes on around mobile-is-the-future discussions. Namely, that "mobile," as an industry, not only includes simple voice and text handsets—the kind of phone you probably had a decade ago—but remains made up predominantly of them. While it's not really in the view of this chapter to cover it, I would be remiss in leaving out this fact as well as mentioning the impressive growth and agility of SMS-based industry throughout the world. It's the most widely used technology on the planet, so much so that it has even been judged a suitable replacement for coin currency in some countries. The financial autonomy and foundation for bootstrapping of all sorts of ventures that SMS has brought to individuals in third-world countries is nothing short of inspiring.[3] I am eagerly awaiting the feedback loop that text messaging will create and its impact upon the way we do things on the web.

To sum this all up, the mobile ecosystem is certainly growing quickly, but it's still early enough to respond calmly to the challenges, if not the sense of urgency, it presents. Mobile strategies characterized by assumptions, panic and a misunderstanding of how the ecosystem is taking shape are prompting far too many to prematurely commit to application development when they should be focusing on the web.

The Case Against Apps

I'm not categorically against apps. On the contrary, I think apps are quite suitable for a variety of purposes; in particular, productivity, gaming, communications and one-way, consumable media are all types of applications that work quite well in the mobile context. But apps are not an ideal format for wide and unmonetized content distribution. In addition to a format mismatch, the economic and practical factors surrounding the creation and distribution of the apps themselves are, in my opinion, indicators that the long-term sustainability of the app paradigm is unlikely. I have three main complaints in my case against apps.

1. Economic Oligarchy

The charge of economic oligarchy is, admittedly, more of a political complaint I have with the way in which the overall apps marketplace has been established. But in that it is political, I feel that it fundamentally contributes to the imbalance and unsustainability of the apps economy. Presently, there are only two companies that control almost the entirety of consumer app-related commerce: Apple and Google. And while scores of developers are understandably excited about their 70 percent cut of the revenue generated by the sale of their applications, the economic conditions will always remain drastically in favor of the very tippy top.

At the time I last investigated, there were more than nine hundred thousand unique mobile applications available for download. That's a staggering number considering the relative recency of the launch of the two app marketplaces, which, by the way, have already seen more than twenty-eight billion downloads combined. The activity and the revenue have reached far beyond anyone's expectations. Since there's so much money to spread around, all the application designers and developers must be doing quite well, right? Not exactly. Consider this: The average price of a mobile app is a paltry $3.64. Only an unusually prolific individual could expect to get rich developing apps, whereas the owner of the entire marketplace has only to open the doors, so to speak, to generate significant wealth. Additionally, Apple and Google have tight control over which apps make it into their inventory. These factors result in a system that is not exactly an innovation breeding ground. The real innovation has already happened—the creation of the marketplace itself. The next big thing is much more likely to come from outside the app marketplace (like, say, on the web), where fewer controls exist to stifle such things.

2. Unnecessary Redundancy

If you are a designer or developer, the pain of inefficiency should resonate with you, even if you have never created a mobile app. Because of the platform division between the two major marketplaces, not to mention others like the Windows Phone and Amazon Kindle Fire, developers are forced to build their mobile apps several times in order to make them available to the largest number of potential users. The Apple and Android platforms are proprietary systems with unique technical requirements. Economic competition, of course, is the only real reason for this—and, in my opinion, it is not a good enough reason to validate the resulting doubling, tripling or quadrupling of effort. Surely there are plenty of competitive angles that could be pushed as far as the devices themselves are concerned (e.g., form factor, feature sets and network carriers) that a standardized approach to app development could be possible. But for now, that is not the case. It's not only the developers that suffer under these conditions. If I were considering green-lighting the production of a mobile app, I would be frustrated enough by having to fund essentially the same thing twice to consider it a legitimate barrier to entry. It is only a matter of time before that pressure results in developers either limiting their capabilities to one platform or the other (which, in and of itself might make sense—Michael Surtees, a principal of Gesture Theory, had some thoughts on this that are worth considering),[4] or rebelling en masse and forcing the app dictators to tear down the wall between them (hyperbole intended). My hope, of course, is for the latter.

3. No URLs

As a web enthusiast, the lack of URLs for apps and the information they contain is my biggest complaint against the app marketplace. Without a protocol for locating the information contained within an app, its ability to be found and shared is nonexistent. Here's just one example: WIRED was one of the first major publications to release an iPad app version of its magazine. I eagerly anticipated trying it out after seeing many demo videos and generally buying into the hype that preceded it. When it did finally launch in May of 2010, I immediately looked it up in the Apple App Store, paid the $3.99 for the first issue and waited several minutes for it to download. I spent some time "flipping" through it, but it was not long before I gave in to disappointment—you know, the kind that you deny for a while in order to avoid the sting of shame that comes from naive capitulation to undeserved hype. Yes, I thought it was going to be wonderful. No, it was not. The main reason? No URLs!

The *Wired* app has a nifty time-line interface that lets you "zoom out" to see all the articles contained in an individual issue. It's a nice UI idea, and not a bad way to navigate the issue on a tablet. But suppose I read an article in the issue and then wanted to share it with with a friend or among my social network. There is really no good way to do so; the article itself doesn't have a specific address of its own, nor does the issue as a whole. The best I could do would be to link to *Wired* Magazine's listing at iTunes.[5] The article I read is an undifferentiated, unlocatable piece of the issue—the 500 MB glorified PDF that we're calling an "app." Sadly, this is not just a hypothetical scenario; this very conundrum presented itself to me within an hour of downloading that first issue. Being the savvy and resourceful web user that I am, I went to www.wired.com, found the article I liked and sent a link to that URL—the web version—to my friend. Just a second or two later, after clicking "Send," I thought, *Why didn't I just start here in the first place?* You know, on the web—where, for the most part, the exact same content offered by the $3.99 app is available for free, along with additional sharing and engagement opportunities the app version lacks.

This is my central objection to "appified" versions of content that have a more natural, flexible and indexable incantation on the web. Rushing to hop on the mobile app bandwagon has resulted in a thoughtless trend of cramming content into impenetrable shells. If you searched for information that would best be supplied by content in a mobile app, you wouldn't find it with Google. (And sadly, you would be just as unlikely to find it using Apple's App Store search tool, which falls far short of being useful.) But you would find it in plenty on the web. For those creating content simply to share or for marketing purposes—as a means of describing expertise and educating prospects about a product or service that could be useful to them—the locating and sharing limitations of apps undermine the very purpose of content, whereas the inherent nature of the web provides the platform upon which it can fulfill it.

Between the economic factors, the practical inefficiencies of development and the lack of URLs, apps are currently subject to a system that almost seems intent on stunting the potential of content. Of course, looking at the sales numbers of mobile apps, you might not think anything was wrong. I certainly don't want to rain on anyone's parade, but something is wrong when the outcome falls far short of the promise. When it comes to apps, we should be clear in admitting where they lack many of the things that make the web great.

The Case for the Web

If apps are not the best format for content, then how does one account for mobile technology in a comprehensive digital strategy? My belief is that the web provides a strong answer by naturally accounting for the weaknesses of apps in its most basic attributes. In particular, there are three web-centric principles that can provide strong guidance as you are assembling a mobile approach.

1. Content First, Context Second

Most of the conversations we have with our clients about mobile technology involve planning for how to account for existing web content in an overall mobile strategy. The key point here is that, in the context of these discussions, the existing content has already proven itself and there is a recognized need to extend its accessibility across wider conditions—namely, to mobile users. But invariably, as we work on adapting content templates for mobile devices, we start getting requests to build new types of unique content—essentially separate, mobile-specific versions of websites. That's where the logic gets unproductively circular—why are we all of the sudden talking about creating new, unique content when the entire conversation started around making the existing content easier to consume for mobile users? If we were to take that route (for which there could be good reasons), the new content would be untested—a risk. But the existing content has already met the demand test. That is why mobile strategy should proceed from content, not the other way around.

By the way, this principle extends to particular technologies, as they can become a barrier, too. For instance, video, which might generally be accessible on the web implemented with Adobe Flash-based players, won't work on most mobile devices. The solution, of course, isn't necessarily to create new video content. Rather, it should be to facilitate wider accessibility to the existing video content by choosing the right technology that works in all contexts. YouTube is a good solution for this.

2. Use Unique URLs

I hope I already made clear why a lack of URLs is a weakness of apps. On the web, the question of where a piece of content exists is almost always relevant—to the humans that search for it, interact with it, share it and save it for later, as well as to the search engine bots that crawl the web indexing it. In short, addresses matter. Imagine if you went to visit a friend at an apartment building but did not have their apartment number. The best you could do would be to knock on every door on every floor until you found the right one. We take this for granted on the web, but had there not been a web version of the *Wired* article I mentioned earlier, I would have had no way to direct anyone else to it.

In January 2011, Mathew Ingram, a writer for *GigaOM*, was interviewed[6] for an episode of CBC Radio's *Spark* podcast about this very issue and had this to say:

… apps as individual, controlled experiences are good for some things. I'm pretty convinced it's not the best thing for things that have to do with media, with content. The whole lifeblood of content is the sharing, the linking. Whether it's apps or websites, if you look at the ones that don't do that I think you quite quickly come to the realization that they're missing something fundamental.

I completely agree.

3. Create Seamless Experiences

The first priority for creating content in a long-term digital strategy should be to facilitate seamless user experiences across a variety of contexts, from desktop to tablet to smartphone. A working example of this comes from Google Books (I first considered this in a blog post I wrote in March, 2011),[7] which successfully preserves the essential reading experience regardless of the device you use. It is difficult to express how incredible and revolutionary that really is—that I can read a bit on my desktop and pick up exactly where I left off on my tablet or phone without giving any thought at all to bookmarking. Google has made seamlessness innate to their books experience. Of course, the book itself is closer in nature to an app like the *Wired* magazine example, in that it is one file without a master URL or locations for individual chapters or pages. But, it still serves as a great standard to strive for in terms of seamlessness of use. Just imagine what that could mean for content on the web that is truly optimized for reading. I'm confident that we will be able to bring the same level of fluidity to all web content in the not-too-distant future. In fact, that is what the responsive web design movement is all about.

Responsive Web Design

If you are unfamiliar with what *responsive* means as far as web design is concerned, a recent *Design Shack* article by Joshua Johnson provides a useful explanation. The article shows how responsive web design works by employing CSS media queries to reorganize page elements based upon the maximum screen resolution available to the user.[8] Johnson goes into a bit more depth by citing a specific example—the charming site of Meagan Fisher, http://owltastic.com, which has up to five different layout options based upon maximum resolutions of 960 to 480 pixels—and reviewing the CSS and media queries that make its flexibility possible.

This approach certainly makes a lot of sense given the technical issues at play, and it provides a proactive solution for ensuring usability across a wide (and growing) array of contexts. But it is also likely to challenge the process that many designers and clients are used to right now. I can imagine that going through traditional rounds of design to determine how a page will look on screens of differing resolutions—especially once you surpass more than just a couple of options—would be too costly and inefficient to make sense for most projects. It seems that the final, approved design would have to instead provide standards and enable the developer to have latitude for reorganizing and redistributing content based upon an agreed set of priorities within a more iterative process. Because this approach is so new, there are likely to be a multitude of practices for integrating responsive design into project work flows. I am on the lookout for an effective, tried-and-true process that can be scaled across projects of significantly different scopes. Ethan Marcotte's book, *Responsive Web Design*[9], is the best source I know of at this early stage in the progress of these new techniques, though the developers at my firm have not yet fully integrated them into our process. In the meantime, they have been exploring techniques for providing alternate templates and style sheets that reformat existing website content for mobile users,[10] which is a step toward the responsive method that still allows us to follow more traditional design and approval procedures with our clients and partners. Mobile is more than just a format; it is a complete paradigm shift. To make the transition feel more secure and manageable to our clients, we've found this intermediate step to be necessary for the time being.

The Future ...

The web is a work in progress. As this is my mantra for all things web, it is not going to be any different with mobile. While we are not quite at the level of seamlessness that Google Books offers, that level will one day be possible and is certainly a decent standard to strive for even now.

THE WEB OF
TOMORROW

No book about the web would be complete without

taking some time to imagine its future. But results may vary: Imagining the future of the web is less an exercise in prediction as it is a chance to raise important questions.

Will the Web Last?

If we were to take as big a step back as possible, one relevant question might be whether the web will exist at all for much longer. The idea that the web is vulnerable to obsolescence created by a current or future technology isn't that wild. Plenty of serious thinkers acknowledge its relative fragility as compared with other, far more enduring technologies. Some even believe it is in decline, if not already dead, as Chris Anderson announced in a provocative issue of *Wired* magazine in the spring of 2010.[1] On the other hand, though the web is still quite "young," it may have more endurance than its eulogists assume.[2] That is certainly my opinion. With such a deep level of cultural and economic immersion, it seems far more likely that the web will continue to endure, if not grow, than to be so quickly snuffed out by the advent of a new competing technological or cultural stream.

In its short time, the web has transformed from an experiment into an industry, from employing people intellectually to employing people economically. The significance of this cannot be overlooked. In the first decade of the web, early adopters were essentially experimenting with the viability of the web as a new way to communicate, learn and entertain, if not a replacement for other, outdated means. Because those initial experiments were so successful, enthusiasm spread, new habits were formed and many web-based versions of things like letter writing, document creation and organization, data analysis, voice communication, audio and video entertainment, journalism and much, much more radically expanded the reach and volume of the web as a communications technology. With the web now engaging the active participation and employment of millions of people, the internet—remember, the web and the internet are two separate but codependent things—has taken its place alongside other civic utilities like water, heat and electricity and, like them, is too essential to human livelihood to ignore. Of course, having secured a place within human infrastructure comes at a cost in flexibility and agility. Wide, sweeping changes to the system—whether the facilities and hardware driving the Internet or the structure of its information in the web of information it conveys—are not likely to be made quickly now that so many social, economic and even political factors rely upon its stability. In other words, to whatever extent those millions for whom the web is valuable can, they will almost certainly work to keep it going.

How Will the Web Change?

As for how the future of the web will actually look, that is another question altogether, one that is far too difficult to predict with certainty. Even though we understand "the web" and "the internet" in general, each is actually made possible by many distinct technologies, within which the number of variables to consider as future factors is almost uncountable. Though web technology is often seen as monolithic—a singular course of development that can be tracked and predicted—it is, in reality, ecosystemic. The developments in hardware, software and information all progress on different, albeit parallel, tracks. And within the technological ecosystem of the web, of course, exist its users, who have their own shaping effect upon the trajectory of technological change. In fact, it is their involvement, through use and creative innovation en masse, that has created an unprecedented compression of technological change. Never before have we created so much so quickly. Forecasting in this kind of environment is, to say the least, a challenge. Instead of attempting to predict specific outcomes, it may be a wiser preparation for the future to examine several potentialities and the questions they raise.

As any good forecast depends upon an understanding of the past, we should first review the history of the web, paying particular attention to the key ideas and innovations that made it possible. What will become clear is that there are two distinct threads to this history—one having to do with the nature of information and the other with how we transmit it—that converge with the creation of the web.

A (Very) Short History of the Web

Let's start with Sputnik. Though it may not immediately appear related, the launch of Sputnik in 1957 is a landmark event in the web's biography. Besides being one of the most significant technological achievements of the twentieth century, the Russian satellite was a catalyst for a decade of rapid-fire development in communications technology in the United States and England. The truth is that Sputnik caught us off guard in a major way. The United States was unaware of even the possibility of being leapfrogged by the Russians, so when Soviet projects claimed first place for successfully putting a man-made object into orbit around the Earth and then launching the first living creature (the poor Laika,[3] who did not return to tell the tale) into space, they began moving much faster. Less than one year later, the United States had formed the Advanced Research Projects Agency (known today as DARPA after adding Defense to it), which funded and organized some of the most significant thinkers in the web's family tree. Without the work done in the years immediately following to conceive of and construct networks that would become the Internet, there would have been no infrastructure within which to create the first links of the web.

In the early sixties, DARPA researcher J.C.R. Licklider began packing radically grand new ideas of human-computer symbiosis and what he called the "Intergalactic Computer Network" into relatively brief papers.[4] The terms with which he imagined the technological ubiquity of our future have since been recognized as seminal to historians of the Internet and are indicative of our ability to turn dreams into expectations. Within the next few years, *packet switching*, a method of breaking information into smaller pieces, distributing them across a network at variable rates determined by the overall traffic volume and reassembling them at their destination, was simultaneously discovered by two researchers: Paul Baran in the United States and Donald Davies in the United Kingdom.[5] Often compared to organic systems, such as the communication and work distribution of ant colonies, packet switching allows the most efficient of many possible routes between points in a network to emerge based upon existing traffic. If we imagine the internet of the late sixties as similar to an early road system, packet switching was the technology that would enable it to successfully scale once everyone had a car. In a paper written toward the end of that incredible decade, Lawrence Roberts described how resource-sharing computer networks could use packet switching to increase output and efficiency beyond anything seen before.[6] Today, as we can hardly envision any other way of working with information, this is an insight we almost certainly take for granted. Every email, instant message, text message or data transfer of any kind across the Internet depends upon these concepts.

Though the prospect of technological inferiority was evidently an adequate motivator for the accomplishments of the DARPA researchers in the years after Sputnik, it doesn't sufficiently explain the origins of the ideas that supported their work. Licklider, Baran, Davies and Roberts were unequivocally brilliant, yet none would have claimed that their work was truly novel. They probably would have attributed their successes to unprecedented investment in time and resources, which, in turn, enabled them to finally explore and realize work that had its inception in the thinking of others who predated them. Each of their innovations pursued an already existing but unachieved idea: decentralizing information.

Over a decade before the DARPA projects even began, Vannevar Bush had anticipated the unique direction that information technology would take, though it was unconsidered by his contemporaries. As John Lienhard points out, when "everyone else was still predicting fast cars, rocket transportation and personal helicopters," Bush "foresaw credit cards, bar codes, even the Internet. But he saw it all in analog form. He missed the digital revolution."[7] He recognized that the most ambitious innovations would come in the form of information technology, and he most famously imagined a device that would organize and make accessible to its operator an enormous library of information compressed using microfilm technology. As a microcosm of the future Internet, Bush's device, which he called the *memex*, would not be a node in a larger system—in the way that we access the web using today's computers—but the entire system itself. The user would gather and store information, which without significant limitations could conceivably exceed any library he or she would otherwise have access to. But in his article written for the *Atlantic Monthly* titled "As We May Think"[8], Bush stressed the real value of the device:

> All this is conventional, except for the projection forward of present-day mechanisms and gadgetry. It affords an immediate step, however, to associative indexing, the basic idea of which is a provision whereby any item may be caused at will to select immediately and automatically another. This is the essential feature of the memex. The process of tying two items together is the important thing. When the user is building a trail, he names it, inserts the name in his code book, and taps it out on his keyboard. Before him are the two items to be joined, projected onto adjacent viewing positions. At the bottom of each there are a number of blank code spaces, and a pointer is set to indicate one of these on each item. The user taps a single key, and the items are permanently joined. In each code space appears the code word. Out of view, but also in the code space, is inserted a set of dots for photocell viewing; and on each item these dots by their positions designate the index number of the other item.
>
> Thereafter, at any time, when one of these items is in view, the other can be instantly recalled merely by tapping a button below the corresponding code space. Moreover, when numerous items have been thus joined together to form a trail, they can be reviewed in turn, rapidly or slowly, by deflecting a lever like that used for turning the pages of a book. It is exactly as though the physical items had been gathered together from widely separated sources and bound together to form a new book. It is more than this, for any item can be joined into numerous trails.

Knowing what we now know about the grand scale of the world's information and the possibilities for accessing it once resources are shared—as Lawrence Roberts later imagined—the memex would certainly not impress today's web users. After all, Bush didn't imagine a network of memexes.

There would have been far more unavailable to a memex operator than available, and the serendipity of discovery that we take for granted on the web today would not have been a part of the experience. However, as a curatorial device for information already relevant to the user, its power was in the ease of storage and recall—a compelling notion for those used to often being an inconvenient distance from the information they needed. From today's perspective, both its limitations and its novelty are clear. The amount of information available and, more important, the human appetite for information, secured the obsolescence of the memex almost immediately. Yet, the idea that its user could build a conceptually interconnected system of information—a taxonomy that meant something to them—and recall from its storage any bit of information on the basis of related ideas was new and would take decades to reappear in the form of the tagging systems so common today. Bush's memex was, literally, an analog to today's web.

Just like the DARPA group, Bush, too, owed a debt to forefathers in thought. In particular, the core three ideas of the memex—miniaturizing information using microfilm, consolidating the world's information and storing it in one central location, and using a conceptual framework to navigate information—all appear to have an origin in the work of two French researchers working far earlier. In the early 1890s, Paul Otlet and Henri La Fontaine began what would become decades of collaborations on a variety of projects having to do with information theory.[9] Sharing backgrounds in law and an interest in the study of books, Otlet and La Fontaine sought to expand the notion of information beyond what they considered to be the limitations of the book. Among their many experiments that have apparent modern counterparts, three in particular—exploring taxonomy, centralization and miniaturization—are important ancestors of the web. The duo even created a service to answer questions via mail.

Almost immediately after beginning work together, Otlet and La Fontaine began to study the American Dewey Decimal System and discuss ways to expand its scope as a classification tool. Even before they had a proof of concept in place, Otlet thought to secure permission from Melvil Dewey to modify his work. Dewey agreed, but with the provision that

Otlet and La Fontaine keep their work on their side of the Atlantic. By 1907, Otlet and La Fontaine had published a proposal for a new system, one that introduced an algebraic expression for indicating compound classifications rather than simply increasing the number of classes possible in Dewey's system. This had never been done before. Rather than forcing a book that covers multiple concepts (e.g., technology, design and the web) to be organized under one category, the Universal Decimal Classification included a provision for each concept in its numeric system. Like tagging an article with multiple tags, a book could be classified with multiple subjects.

A few years later, the pair imagined a physical application of their new system. Initially dubbed the "city of knowledge," Otlet and La Fontaine secured funding from the Belgian government to construct a large-scale collection of information entered on index cards and organized with the Universal Decimal Classification. As the collection grew, Otlet renamed it the Mundaneum and expanded it to include a wider variety of media, such as files, reports, letters, articles and images. Though its goal of gathering and organizing the world's information was ultimately as futile as Bush's memex, it certainly got closer. The Mundaneum housed 15 million index cards, one hundred thousand files, and millions of images. Among those images were also some of the earliest examples of bibliographic microfilm. Otlet had been involved in experiments with other researchers to use the relatively new technique of microphotography to capture, compress and store information from books, and much of that material, including his attempt to create a complete microfilm encyclopedia, became part of the Mundaneum.

The goals of these early innovations sound uncannily like contemporary projects still in progress on the web. In particular, it is remarkable that the current frenzy of activity around enabling and economizing the transition of books from the page to the screen is still underway over a century after its start with Otlet's microfilm work. The question of why this goal, having been set over a century ago, has taken so long to come to fruition has a complex answer that, in and of itself, could fill its own book. Certainly resistance from various industries, in the form of the same self-preservation of large systems that the web is likely to employ in the coming years, not to mention the practical limitations of time and energy to transfer every book from one format to another, I suspect have much to do with it. But at the heart of the distance between the work of Otlet, La Fontaine and Bush and today's web is a conceptual leap in understanding, from thinking of information in terms of its physical manifestation to its incorporeal essence. As long as information remained trapped in physical representations—in entries printed on index cards, collections of files, slides of microfilm and other images, or of course books and other documents—any collection of it could only really be a very small piece of the total information available in the world. In other words, information needs to make the transition from books to bits.

The work of DARPA brought the incorporeality of information, which had its own long history of thought reaching as far back as Plato, into practical reality.[10] With every bit conveyed by the Internet, we began to understand and experience the transit of information in a revolutionary new way. But it was the work of Tim Berners-Lee that employed DARPA's system to create something that more closely resembled what Otlet, La Fontaine and Bush imagined. Tim Berners-Lee's World Wide Web experiment connected the concepts and inventions that preceded him, demonstrating the incorporeality of information in a way that anyone could understand by using it. Rather than information printed on paper, his experimental web pages were information displayed on screens. And unlike Otlet, La Fontaine and Bush, who thought that this display would be a projected picture of printed pages, Berners-Lee's pages were entirely new, based upon a programming language that processed bits of information sent over the Internet's network and displayed them in a visually controllable way. A book, which might occupy 120 printed pages and physical space on a shelf, could now be miniaturized to an almost imperceivable degree, yet displayed on a screen intelligibly. With this kind of power, assembling the world's information, a grandiose and impossible task in Otlet's day, was now within reach.

Everything We Do Today Will Change

In the decades since the birth of the web, this is what we have been doing: creating and organizing the world's "library" in electronic format. The existence of entirely new industries, particularly those built around search technology, are indicative of our success so far. Google, one of today's most influential companies worldwide, began as an experiment to represent an organizational method in an algorithm. Because it worked so well, more people were able to access the web's information and contribute to it in new ways. Google became like oil in the gears of an unimaginably complex machine, enabling thousands to make their livings creating new information as well as translating existing information from analog formats to digital ones accessible on the web. Having secured the dependence of almost every web user with its search, advertising, email, productivity and analytics tools, Google continues to work on one of Otlet and La Fontaine's goals: to make the world's bibliographic information accessible on screens.

Each of the major points on the timeline that we've looked at—the work of Otlet and La Fontaine, Bush's memex, Sputnik, the advances of DARPA and finally Tim Berners-Lee's invention of the web—could be explored in much greater detail, not to mention further illuminated by filling in the many gaps between them (a necessary caveat for a book like this one). But sometimes the bigger and more complex a story is, the more it needs to be simplified in order for us to grasp its meaning. Even this cursory look at the timeline serves to illustrate that it is the timeline itself that can tell us quite a lot about the future of the web.

The invention of the web is often compared with the invention of the printing press. Both had a radical, sweeping and relatively immediate effect upon human civilization. The printing press provided a mechanism by which literacy could spread at a rate unknown to humanity before, and in doing so, it enabled significant developments in philosophy, the sciences and even liberty. Certainly, the printing press, by virtue of its shaping power over culture, was a prerequisite of the web.

In preparation for a presentation I later gave the employees of my firm on the future of our industry, I plotted every notable development in technology that I could recall prior to the present on a timeline.[11] Once I had marked almost one hundred events, I realized I needed to begin to simplify things—I was really looking for the landmark innovations upon which current (and future) technology rested. After pruning my list, the final count I ended up with was seven. The comparison with the printing press was important to my understanding of the cultural history behind the web, so I made that the first event on my time line and the invention of the web the last. Between them were five other events that were either technological or cultural foundations that I believe are necessary to understanding the web and its future.

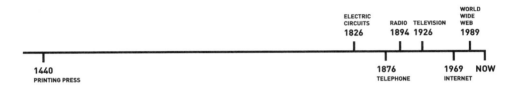

In simplifying the time line, I noticed that a significant increase in entries did not appear for over four hundred years after the printing press. That acceleration of innovation, which included the invention of the telephone, the radio and television (among many other technologies not shown) was actually made possible by the discovery of how to control electricity. Prior to the creation of electric circuits, the understanding of electricity had deepened, yet it was the harnessing of it that powered—literally—the unprecedented speed of technological progress afterward. Though the world of the early twenty-first century would be almost unrecognizable to the late-eighteenth-century citizens for whom the lights had just been turned on, the time line makes clear how new, and therefore potentially unstable, the web truly is. Roughly two decades separated the telephone and radio, three radio and television, and four television and the Internet. Compared with the centuries between the printing press and controlled electricity, these time spans are not only brief, but virtually indistinct. If only twenty years have passed since the invention of the web, and only forty since the invention of the technology through which the web is made possible—the internet—it is reasonable to expect the web itself to continue to evolve in significant ways.

But what if the time scale was increased even further? As I reflected upon the story this time line began to tell, I wondered how it might change if the time line included other important events in the history of communication technology. Though, again, many could be included, I limited my entries to two additional events—the creation of writing and the invention of the codex, which bound pages together like the books we know today—prior to the invention of the printing press. Because the scale of my time line had to change to accommodate a much vaster expanse of time, I simplified the entries after the printing press down to only one: the web. Had the other entries for the electric circuit, the telephone, radio, television and the Internet remained, you would need a magnifying glass to see them!

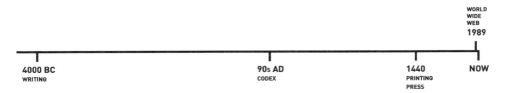

WORLD WIDE WEB 1989

4000 BC
WRITING

90s AD
CODEX

1440
PRINTING PRESS

NOW

Illustrating the story in this way, by "zooming out" as it were, we can see that the progress of communications technology, from the first writing to today, was even slower. The largest gap in this time line is over ten times as long as in the previous time line. It was over four thousand years after the earliest writing before humans discovered that the documents they created could be organized differently—from on discreet surfaces like stone or wax tablets and scrolls to collections bound together in a book. After the codex, it was another thirteen hundred years or so until the printing press provided the technology to replace the slow and painstaking process of hand-copying texts. In light of the millennia leading up to the printing press, it's no wonder it had the impact it did. And yet, we've grown accustomed to a pace unimaginable to Gutenberg's contemporaries. This is a handy thing to keep in mind when you find yourself impatiently waiting for that document to print at work—you know, the one you sent wirelessly from your computer to the printer? In the fifteenth century, that would have taken a few days of work and come at a very high cost.

Almost 550 years passed between the printing press and the web, 80 percent of which, as we saw in the first time line, had very little development. The bigger the scope of the story, the more the spans of time representing our progress expand before the printing press and contract after it. On this second time line, the creation of the web looks even newer than before. It's humbling, really, which puts us in the right frame of mind from which to imagine the future. Hubris makes for poor prediction.

The insight that this research brought was exactly what I wanted my presentation to communicate: The web, the very reason my firm exists, predates my firm by only five years! We've adapted as the web has changed—small fluctuations compared with the grander scheme of technology, but great for an industry based upon a single thread of technology. We've learned to become better at what we do and better at predicting the shifts. But that process is certainly not over. The rapid change of ideas and technology that brought us to the present, which we can see more soberly than ever thanks to these time lines, should remind us that the way was paved by the clustering of many new ideas and enabling technology resulting from previous ones. What we conceive of today—what we think the web is and the best ways to use it—coming from only twenty years of relatively small idea clusters, iterative technological development and a whole lot of trial and error, will change. Kevin Kelly, referencing his own diagrams of technological progress included in his book *What Technology Wants*,[12] nonetheless provides a perfect caption for my time lines, encapsulating the zeitgeist they reveal:

These charts capture a feeling we have that change is accelerating even within our own lifetimes. Novelty arrives in a flash (compared to earlier), and there seems to be a shorter and shorter interval between novel changes. Technologies get better, cheaper, faster, lighter, easier, more common, and more powerful as we move into the future.

Reviewing the history of the web makes clear that the clustering of ideas that made it possible is a phenomenon that continues today, but with growing complexity. This makes the particularities of the web's future difficult, if not impossible, to reliably predict.[13] But it can be said with great likelihood that everything we do today, as far as the internet and the web are concerned, will change.

Potential Change Agents

Up to this point, the web has predominantly been about us. Whether we've used it to create or consume content, the thrust of our activity has been characterized by self-involvement: what we think, what we are doing, what we want.

In this way, the web is like a diary, one to which we collectively add our passing thoughts, greatest secrets, plans for the future and, well, anything and everything else that comes to mind. But few diarists keep it up for the long term. While there are plenty of examples of life-long diarists, the majority—you, perhaps; I, certainly—have seen their productive times interrupted by often longer bouts of silence. Perhaps life settles down in these gaps, leaving little that seems worthy of an entry, or, on the other hand, an increase in stress or excitement just leaves little energy left to spend time writing it all down. In either case, diary fatigue is a thing. So I wonder, is there no reason to think that web fatigue could also become a thing? Will the web need to become more than a mirror to hold our interest?

It is ironic that as the gathering momentum of self-expression-enabling technologies has, as Douglas Rushkoff points out, finally caught us up with the ethos of the printing press, our interest may actually be on the wane.[14] For the first time in history, anyone can publish—anytime they like—and yet the urgent question of the day is whether they will. As internet access and web literacy peak, those on the innovative and creative edge—those who blogged before blogging and tweeted before tweeting—may begin to explore entirely new ways of expressing themselves. Maybe they'll start writing letters again.

That is, unless the economy beats them to it. Economic factors may preempt boredom, eroding the individual's sense of ownership and freedom over the web before they have a chance to give up on it themselves. What began as an experiment in expression through a new medium has evolved far beyond the experimental. It has become essentially human. The 2009 closing of GeoCities, one of the earliest communities established on the web, marked the end of the experimental phase.[15] At its start, the residents of GeoCities were offered a free place to publish their content and were organized into thematic neighborhoods—a metaphor that created a sense of local intimacy despite the reality that neighbors might physically reside thousands of miles apart. The freedom to publish and to build virtual communities, and to do so based upon mutual interest, were all new and exciting in 1995. Seeing an opportunity to profit from this new culture, Yahoo purchased GeoCities four years later. Not surprisingly, the citizens of GeoCities began to move away.

One might argue that the borders of GeoCities were already eroding, that a boundary established on the basis of a distant novelty will inevitably cease to exist in any meaningful way. But the balance of culture and economics is precarious, to say nothing of the muddy causal relationship between the two. Was the homogenization of GeoCities culture what put it on Yahoo's purchase radar in the first place? Or was privatization to blame for GeoCities' folk skipping town? The answer is certainly debatable. What is clear is that a culture once particular to a small corner of the web had successfully spread and become integral to the web at large.

This phenomenon continues today, but on a much broader scale. By creating a new "natural" resource in content, the web has been radically commercially disruptive. Once a finely controlled product created by a minority—those few who had the time and resources to do so—content is now a commodity, and an abundant one at that. Naturally, companies have been desperate to find ways of quelling the disruption by controlling the production of that commodity and monetizing it. Of course, this is a greatly simplified summary of what has happened, but distilling it in this way does raise valid questions: Why do we create? What do we hope to gain from it? Web users may be willing to trade novelty—and it's accompanying instability—for the predictable stability of a corporatized web, but if what they create is controlled and turned into a product from which they see no benefit, they may see that exchange quite differently. Boredom alone may be a considerable cultural obstacle to maintaining the status quo on the web, but economic factors compound the challenge.

If boredom shifts web culture in a new direction before companies have successfully co-opted it, the resulting innovation could again create disruption and steer the economy of the web in a new direction—a win for users in principle, but perhaps not if it upsets the market too greatly.[16] On the other hand, boredom could have the opposite effect: Rather than creating new innovation, it could create complacency—the kind that, in light of the uphill struggle required to do something new, acquiesces to the powers that make it far easier to play by their rules. The market may win in that scenario, and the web may stagnate. It's a finely balanced equation.

From Us to Our Stuff

In the meantime, there are existing technological threads that hint at new ways the internet and the web can be used. But my concern with some of them is that though the technologies are solid, the ideas grounding their use are not.

Take Augmented Reality (AR) as an example. AR is essentially a data-enhanced view of the world around us made visible through applications like Layar, a mobile browser that uses your phone's compass, GPS and accelerometer to project data relevant to your location over its camera's view. If you've never used an AR application, imagine what walking a city block might look like to a cyborg. The cyborg is you; the view, yours also, as long as you're willing to reduce it to a palm-sized rectangle. While an initial AR experience can be thrilling, it quickly becomes clear, especially to visual thinkers, that AR is a misapplication of the technology currently at our disposal. AR is disappointing precisely because it is so visual.

Kevin Slavin, in a recent presentation he called "Reality Is Plenty, Thanks"[17] pointed out that limiting our field of view—not to mention flooding our newly downsized vista with visual data displays—can actually be dangerous. Citing an automotive study that found that AR displays for drivers placed them in greater danger than those who did not use them, Slavin homed in on the counterintuitive relationship between information and our apprehension of reality: More can sometimes be less. By projecting a synthetic data stream—the kind we're used to receiving at our desks—over our real-time view of the world, we create a quasi reality and disable ourselves in the process. We cut ourselves off from the real world and its expansive data stream—the kind we're accustomed to sensing through sound, touch and our peripheral vision. AR, though it may trick the eye into believing otherwise, is in the end one-dimensional. It will fail for the same reason its predecessor, Virtual Reality, failed: The mind can only suspend so much disbelief, especially when it's trying to be productive. Slavin concludes that AR, insofar as it is representative of a noble goal to enhance the perception of reality, "might not best be expressed by making anything you look at."

On that note, I'm with Slavin. We already know that information is everywhere; seeing it on screens only creates more work for us to do. For the boredom prone, especially, this is not a sustainable proposition. But if a machine can collect and deliver data to our eyes, it should also be able to save us the trouble of analyzing and interpreting them. It is in interpretation that the true value of technology that can sense, store, analyze and predict lies. This stuff—let's call it awareness technology—should be doing much more for us than making advertising more ubiquitous. It should be helping us do more work, more efficiently and more effectively. So, rather than trying to enhance how we see reality, we should instead consider augmenting reality for machines. A more aware machine is far more valuable to us than a more crowded visual field.

Rapid progress is being made in developing awareness technology right now (don't worry, not the sort of dystopian robot overlord stuff of science fiction). Though significant, the practical developments in this field are, for the most part, unseen and therefore unnoticed by most of us. Radio-frequency Identification (RFID) is just one example of an open and rapidly scalable awareness tool already in use for a wide variety of purposes. Because they don't need to be seen—literally—to be read, RFIDs can be miniaturized and embedded in just about anything in order to build networks of information among objects. Right now, cars, roads, tollbooths, tickets, library books, passports, product packaging, casino chips, cattle, machine parts—the list alone could fill this page—are being enhanced by RFIDs for such a broad diversity of purposes that only your imagination could impose a limit. But what's the benefit of building an internet of things?

Consider this scenario: Every wastebasket in your city is fit with sensors that measure its capacity and send data back to a central repository. As the database grows, algorithms are run to analyze capacity data, identify patterns and predict when and where wastebaskets will be full. New pickup routes can now be plotted on the fly, likely saving what is, in the aggregate, a lot of wasted time and fuel. Just recently, I watched a garbage truck go through the motions of emptying several already empty dumpsters as I walked to work. A networked system would have prevented that. They may not sound glamorous, but smart sanitation systems are the type of practical, efficiency-gaining, energy-saving application of awareness technology that will be in extraordinary demand over the next decade. If you can envision and implement a scenario like this one, you'll also be granted latitude to dream up applications that are far more creative and inspiring to you. Although, what could be more inspiring than designing a city that works?

If today's web is about us, tomorrow's web will be about our stuff. Not just our individual possessions, but bigger things, like our homes, our cities, our entire infrastructure. But in the meantime, the names we choose for these future possibilities rarely seem adequate. The internet of things, for example, sounds cute but implies an unlikely separation from the existing Internet as well as the world around it. Russell Davies has suggested a slightly modified alternative: the internet with things.[18] With that adjustment, I think he's getting a bit closer. But any name we choose will limit the scope of what we imagine. Sometimes that's helpful, but in this case, I think that the names underestimate what this next step for the internet could be.

Beyond just indexing things, the future could see the role of the web evolve into something far more profound, something it has yet to accomplish: making the transition from a cultural artifact to a civilizational tool that enriches the physical world with virtual systems, rather than simply projecting images amidst us.

Design students are already looking toward this future and experimenting with the technologies that will surely shape it. Projects like SoundAffects[19] created by undergraduates at Parsons The New School for Design, explore how everyday data gathered in cities—weather, traffic patterns and the like—can be translated into sound and mined for new understanding. Meanwhile, outside of the academy, innovative small firms—like San Francisco's Stamen, New York's Rockwell Group or the London-based studios, BERG and dentsu[20]—are already producing work for their clients as well as investing in research projects that look much like the sensing city scenario I sketched above—work that dentsu artfully describes as "making future magic." What all of these designers have in common is an intentional and strategic expansion of their approach to design, facilitated by a deeper working knowledge of new sensor, sound and programming technologies.

I don't expect there will be less visual work to do in the future. But, there will be more opportunity for visual people who are prepared to apply their expertise to create a variety of other sensory experiences. Those who will be prepared will have already begun exploring new technologies and designing experiences with them, just as some students and multidisciplinary firms are doing today.

The meaning of design has always been about possibilities, not hard-line definitions. It's important to remember that—perhaps today more than any other time before—as technology pushes the boundaries of our professional identities and challenges the distinctions between designer, engineer and technologist. But, technology is more than just a tool; it's an expression of intent. It is how we shape the world around us and conform it to a vision of how we want to live. So, in considering our futures, we must question how technology will define who we are and what we do. Should technology define what it means to be a designer, or should the progress of technology be designed? I believe we'll find the answers to these questions, but not without participating today in the project of imagining the world we will inhabit tomorrow.

NOTES

Introduction

[1] This quote is originally from a 1955 article in *Harper's Magazine,* which has been archived here: http://harpers.org/archive/1955/03/0006860. I first came upon it in a *New York Times* editorial by Wes Davis, located here: http://www.nytimes.com/2010/06/16/opinion/16davis.html.

[2] The full Princeton definition for strategy is as follows:

(n) scheme, strategy (an elaborate and systematic plan of action)

(n) strategy (the branch of military science dealing with military command and the planning and conduct of a war)

This definition can be found online at: http://wordnetweb.princeton.edu/perl/webwn?s=strategy&sub=Search+WordNet&o2=&o0=1&o8=1&o1=1&o7=&o5=&o9=&o6=&o3=&o4=&h=

1. What Is the Web?

[1] My unscientific survey was conducted using LinkedIn. You can view the results by visiting this link: http://www.linkedin.com/answers?viewQuestion=&questionID=787425&askerID=9505648&akey=GvwxG4ofStn-MjdxezpRPqLfPo4N_yo&hkey=b2mx.

[2] Tim Berners-Lee, "Information Management: A Proposal," W3 Archive, 1989, http://www.w3.org/History/1989/proposal.html (accessed January 18, 2011). Also worth reviewing is Berners-Lee's 2000 book, *Weaving the Web* (New York: Harper, 2000).

[3] I found E.B. Whites letter here: http://www.lettersofnote.com/2011/05/library-is-many-things.html

[4] Frank Rose, *The Art of Immersion: How the Digital Generation Is Remaking Hollywood, Madison Avenue, and the Way We Tell Stories* (New York: W.W. Norton & Company, 2011), 17–18.

[5] Harry McCracken, "Will the Next Web Revolution Leave the U.S. Behind?" *PC World* 20 (December 2007): 15.

[6] For your edification, I invite you to visit Fast Food: Ads vs. Reality: http://thewvsr.com/adsvsreality.htm.

1 I first learned about mood boards from Peyton Crump, one of Viget Labs' design directors, who gave a presentation on them at a Refresh the Triangle event near my office. Tom Osborne, another design director at Viget, published a blog post back in 2008 describing how mood boards work. You can read the post here: http://www.viget.com/inspire/getting-moody/. Since getting introduced to them, my firm has made mood boards a permanent step in our web design process. (Justin Kerr, Newfangled's creative director, published some pros and cons of using mood boards here: http://www.newfangled.com/mood_board_observations.)

2 Most readers of this book will probably not be looking for much more information about the programming side of web development, but for those who are, I recommend the following: W. Jason Gilmore, *Beginning PHP and MySQL: From Novice to Professional* (New York: Apress, 2010).

3 For more information on design application techniques, see: David Sawyer McFarland, *CSS: The Missing Manual* (Sebastopol: O'Reilly Media, 2009).

4 Wideman Comparative Glossary of Project Management Terms, v3.1, s.v. "Quality Assurance," http://www.maxwideman.com/pmglossary/PMG_Q00.htm#Quality%20Assurance (accessed February 7, 2011).

5 I don't know of many quality assurance texts specifically devoted to website development. However, there are many texts that focus on application-testing procedures, which can serve as models for smaller-scale projects. A good place to start would be: Ian Molyneaux, *The Art of Application Performance Testing: Help for Programmers and Quality Assurance* (Sebastopol: O'Reilly Media, 2009).

6 My firm has been experimenting with several browser-testing tools. http://CrossBrowserTesting.com, which can test browser performance and some interactive functionality for any URL you submit, can even generate screenshots of any URL in every current browser simultaneously. We've also used SauceLabs' tools, which you can learn more about at their website: https://saucelabs.com/. If these particular tools aren't what you're looking for, there are plenty of competing options available online. In fact, *Smashing Magazine* published an extensive comparison of cross-browser testing tools, which you can find here: http://www.smashingmagazine.com/2011/08/07/a-dozen-cross-browser-testing-tools/.

7 There is an ongoing debate among developers whether websites should be implemented to gracefully degrade or progressively enhance. Aaron Gustafson wrote an article

exploring this topic for A List Apart in 2008, which you can find here: http://www .alistapart.com/articles/understandingprogressiveenhancement.

[8] Glen Whitman, "The Two Things," CSUN.edu. N.p. 15 June 2004, http://www.csun .edu/~dgw61315/thetwothings.html (accessed January 4, 2011).

[9] I recommend several books that cover managing web development projects:

June Cohen, *The Unusually Useful Web Book* (Berkeley: New Riders, 2003).

Edward B. Farkas, *Managing Web Projects* (New York: CRC Press, 2009).

Tim Frick, *Managing Interactive Media Projects* (Clifton Park: Thomson Delmar Learning, 2007).

3. Your Website Is Not for You

[1] "The Persuaders," PBS/*Frontline*, 2004. http://www.pbs.org/wgbh/pages/frontline/shows/ persuaders/

[2] I wrote an article in 2010 on how web tracking works called "If They Are Watching, Should You Watch, Too?" You can find it here: https://www.newfangled.com/if_they_are_ watching_should_you_watch_too.

[3] Mark Hurst, "Ignore the Customer Experience, Lose a Billion Dollars," GoodExperience .com, April 13, 2011, http://goodexperience.com/2011/04/ignore-the-customer-e.php.

[4] Steve Mulder, with Ziv Yaar, *The User Is Always Right: A Practical Guide to Creating and Using Personas for the Web* (Berkeley: New Riders, 2007).

[5] Steve Krug, *Rocket Surgery Made Easy: The Do-it-Yourself Guide to Finding and Fixing Usability Problems* (Berkeley: New Riders, 2009).

4. Information Architecture

[1] A fairly extensive online catalog of historical photos of the museum's dioramas, can be found here: http://images.library.amnh.org/photos/ptm/browse/1.

[2] The American Museum of Natural History's website has a page dedicated to the diorama I described, which can be viewed here: http://www.amnh.org/exhibitions/dioramas/bear/.

[3] The value of wireframes as a website planning tool is a contentious issue. While my opinion—and the process my firm follows—diminishes their role in preference of interactive prototyping, plenty of respected voices hold differing views. For instance, Dan M. Brown's book, *Communicating Design*, contains an entire page devoted to wireframes, which is a good treatment of the subject:

Dan M. Brown, *Communicating Design: Developing Web Site Documentation for Design and Planning*, Second Edition (Berkely: New Riders Press, 2011).

[4] Eric Holter, founder and former CEO of Newfangled, used this term in his 2001 self-published book, *Client vs. Developer Wars*, which you can find here: http://www.newfangled.com/client_vs__developer_wars, as well as a 2001 article on "Web Development Fallacies," which can be found here: http://www.newfangled.com/website_development_difficulties.

[5] One I recommend often is www.protoshare.com.

[6] The opening sequence of the first part of James Burke's miniseries, *The Day the Universe Changed*, which Burke delivers while a magnificent sun "rises" slowly behind him, illustrates this exact concept perfectly. You can find and watch this for yourself (and the entire series) on YouTube here: http://www.youtube.com/watch?v=UtWVfTiQQW8.

[7] Steve Krug, *Don't Make Me Think: A Common Sense Approach to Web Usability* (Berkeley: New Riders, 2005).

[8] I'd recommend Jakob Nielsen's books, in particular *Designing Web Usability: The Practice of Simplicity* (Berkeley: Peachpit Press, 1999), as a valuable resource on the topic.

[9] For much greater detail on website form design, I recommend Luke Wroblewski's book *Web Form Design: Filling in the Blanks* (New York: Rosenfeld Media, 2008).

[10] Jakob Neilsen published an article detailing his eye-tracking research in 2006, which you can find here: http://www.useit.com/alertbox/reading_pattern.html. It later became a book, published in 2009:

Jakob Nielsen and Kara Pernice, *Eyetracking Web Usability* (Berkeley: New Riders Press, 2009).

[1] This often-quoted line originated in a 1962 essay written by Arthur C. Clarke titled "Hazards of Prophecy: The Failure of Imagination," which was included in a collection of essays titled *Profiles of the Future*, published by Harper & Row in the same year. A posting from Mark Brader to a Google Group on the subject of Clarke's Laws clarifies the source: https://groups.google.com/group/rec.arts.sf.misc/msg/e4185210a85826fc?hl=en&pli=1.

[2] Alexis Madrigal, "Take the Data Out of Dating," *The Atlantic*, December 2010, http://www.theatlantic.com/magazine/archive/2010/12/take-the-data-out-of-dating/8299/ (accessed January 3, 2011).

[3] I have greatly simplified this explanation of Google's PageRank. For a much more thorough analysis of the algorithm (warning, here there be equations!), I recommend starting with the Wikipedia entry on PageRank: http://en.wikipedia.org/wiki/PageRank. Several books also provide great insight into Google, both from a technological standpoint and a cultural one. They are:

Steven Levy, *In the Plex: How Google Thinks, Works, and Shapes our Lives* (New York: Simon & Schuster, 2011).

Siva Vaidhyanathan, *The Googlization of Everything (and Why We Should Worry)* (Berkeley: University of California Press, 2011).

Scott Cleland, *Search and Destroy: Why You Can't Trust Google Inc* (St. Louis: Telescope Books, 2011).

[4] PageRank and search engine results page (SERP) standings are very likely to change over time, which is why I was careful to note "at the time of this writing." However, there are many websites that can help you check the PageRank of any URL, such as: http://www.prchecker.info/check_page_rank.php. But you shouldn't obsess over your website's PageRank, even Google says so: http://googlewebmastercentral.blogspot.com/2011/06/beyond-pagerank-graduating-to.html.

[5] Chris Anderson himself has defended his coining of the phrase, "The Long Tail," in a blog post written in 2005: http://longtail.typepad.com/the_long_tail/2005/05/the_origins_of_.html, but also attributes Clay Shirky with having laid a foundation for it in his 2003 essay, "Power Laws, Weblogs, and Inequality" at http://www.shirky.com/writings/powerlaw_weblog.html. An overview of the concept can, of course, be found at Wikipedia: http://en.wikipedia.org/wiki/Long_Tail.

[6] Eric Holter, founder of Newfangled, recorded a short video explaining how basic SEO works. This video can be found at: https://www.newfangled.com/how_to_do_seo_video.

[7] David Segal, "A Bully Finds a Pulpit on the Web," *New York Times*, November 26, 2010, http://www.nytimes.com/2010/11/28/business/28borker.html (accessed November 26, 2010). Within six months, the owner of DecorMyEyes.com had plead guilty to various charges. Segal revisited the story and published an update in May, 2011.

David Segal, "Online Seller Who Bullied Customers Pleads Guilty," *New York Times*, May 12, 2011, http://www.nytimes.com/2011/05/13/business/13borker.html.

[8] Christopher Butler, "Who Are You Speaking To?" Newfangled.com, October 2009, http://www.newfangled.com/who_are_you_speaking_to (accessed October 31, 2009).

6. Making Sense of the Data

[1] I'm referring to Edward Tufte, author of *The Visual Display of Quantitative Information* and other classic books on information visualization. You can learn more about him and his work at his website: http://www.edwardtufte.com/tufte/.

[2] Many books can help you get up to speed with Google Analytics. Two I'd recommend in particular are:

Justin Cutroni, *Google Analytics* (Sebastopol: O'Reilly Media, 2010).

Avinash Kaushik, *Web Analytics 2.0: The Art of Online Accountability and Science of Customer Centricity* (Berkeley: Sybex, 2009).

[3] Discerning readers may have expected social media to have referred far more traffic than Google Analytics reports. I've been surprised at the low number of referrals shown by these reports as well, especially as it's been my experience that Twitter in particular has become a very active referrer over the last year or so. Google Analytics reports that only 3,109 visits have been referred by Twitter in the course of a year, with only sixty-two of them converting. Having kept a close eye on Twitter activity, I certainly would have guessed a much higher number on both counts. The reason for the discrepancy has to do with the URL-shortening services that are now used to enable users to get the most out of Twitter's 140-character limit. These services create alternate URLs that redirect to the original, longer addresses, but in doing so, the resulting traffic appears to Google Analytics as direct traffic, rather than a referral from the domain on which the shortened URL originated. A detailed description of how this works is available from the Wikipedia entry for "URL Shortening," here: http://en.wikipedia.org/wiki/List_

of_URL_redirection_services. However, some of the most common Twitter tools are now integrated with URL-shortening services. For instance, Tweetdeck automatically shortens URLs using one particular service, Bit.ly. By adding a + to a Bit.ly generated link that was used by *Smashing Magazine* to tweet one of my articles (https://bitly.com/ o39XHu+), I can access a detailed report displaying all kinds of information about the activity generated by it. As it shows, 2,539 people clicked this link alone, either in *Smashing Magazine*'s original Tweet or in someone else's re-Tweet of it. None of this traffic appears among the referral traffic reported by Google Analytics. Tools like this verify the relevance of social media referral activity as well as demonstrate some of the current technical hurdles Google Analytics will need to get over in order to present the most accurate activity data.

7. Content

[1] The number of Google search results for the phrase content strategy changed from 80 million to 105 million within a few months time during the writing of this book. I anticipate the number of results to continue to grow and exceed these estimates by the time this book is published.

[2] Iris Monica Vargas, "Mapping Science," *Seed* magazine (January 2010), http:// seedmagazine.com/content/article/mapping_science/.

[3] Eli Pariser, *The Filter Bubble: What the Internet Is Hiding from You* (New York: Penguin Press, 2011).

[4] Jason Fell, "Just 42 Magazines Saw Ad Page Increases in '08." *FolioMag* (January 2009), http://www.foliomag.com/2009/just-42-magazines-saw-ad-page-increases-08.

[5] I published a blog post at that time that included a photograph of this especially "light" issue of AdAge, which you can find at: http://www.newfangled.com/adage_promotion_ in_a_recession.

[6] Adam Gopnik, "The Information," *New Yorker* (February 2011), http://www.newyorker.com/ arts/critics/atlarge/2011/02/14/110214crat_atlarge_gopnik.

[7] Google's official blog announced updates to their algorithm that were intended to ensure the most relevant search results in a February 2011 post, which you can find here: http://googleblog.blogspot.com/2011/02/finding-more-high-quality-sites-in.html.

Danny Sullivan, who blogs at SearchEngineLand.com, published his analysis of Google's approach to prioritizing high-quality content that same day in a post you can find here:

http://searchengineland.com/google-forecloses-on-content-farms-with-farmer-algorithm-update-66071

In March 2011, Steven Levy, author of the authoritative Google book, *In the Plex*, interviewed Google representatives Amit Singhal and Matt Cutts in a Wired Epicenter blog post. Singhal and Cutts revealed that the 2009 update to the Google algorithm, code named Caffeine, resulted in an exponential increase in indexed content—much of it they described as "shallow." The solution was to enrich the algorithm with parameters that evaluated content qualitatively and release it in an update known internally at Google as "Panda." You can find the interview, which delves into the controversy surrounding this issue, here: http://www.wired.com/epicenter/2011/03/the-panda-that-hates-farms/.

[8] My colleague, Mark O'Brien, succinctly maps out the path from planning to conversions in his book, *A Website that Works: How Marketing Agencies Can Create Business Generating Sites*. You can learn more about his book here: http://www.newfangled.com/a_website_that_works.

[9] Erin Kissane, *The Elements of Content Strategy* (New York: A Book Apart, 2011).

[10] Kristina Halvorson, *Content Strategy for the Web* (Berkeley: New Riders, 2010).

[11] Two books that I would recommend as writing resources are:

William Zinsser, *On Writing Well: The Classic Guide to Writing Nonfiction* (New York: Harper Paperbacks, 2006).

Janice Redish, *Letting Go of the Words: Writing Web Content that Works* (San Francisco: Morgan Kaufmann/Elsevier, 2007).

[12] Here, I am referencing the "iceberg theory," which has been attributed to a passage from *Death in the Afternoon*, by Ernest Hemingway:

"If a writer of prose knows enough of what he is writing about he may omit things that he knows and the reader, if the writer is writing truly enough, will have a feeling of those things as strongly as though the writer had stated them. The dignity of movement of an ice-berg is due to only one-eighth of it being above water. A writer who omits things because he does not know them only makes hollow places in his writing."

You can read more about this in the Wikipedia entry for the iceberg theory, which you can find here: http://en.wikipedia.org/wiki/Iceberg_theory.

8. The Mobile Web

[1] For a much more thorough study of how people are using mobile devices, I recommend:

Rich Ling, New Tech, *New Ties: How Mobile Communication Is Reshaping Social Cohesion* (Cambridge: MIT Press, 2010).

Richard Coyne, *The Tuning of Place: Sociable Spaces and Pervasive Digital Media* (Cambridge: MIT Press, 2010).

[2] Tomi Ahonen, "All the Numbers, All the Facts on Mobile the Trillion-Dollar Industry. Why is Google saying: Put Your Best People on Mobile?" Communities Dominate Brands blog, February 17, 2011, http://communities-dominate.blogs.com/brands/2011/02/all-the-numbers-all-the-facts-on-mobile-the-trillion-dollar-industry-why-is-google-saying-put-your-b.html.

[3] For an in-depth look at how mobile technology is shaping cultures across the entire world, see:

Manuel Castells and others, Mobile Communication and Society: A Global Perspective (Cambridge: MIT Press, 2009).

For a very high-level look at the technologies supporting mobile computing, see:

Mark Grayson, Kevin Shatzkamer, and Klass Wierenga, *Building the Mobile Internet* (Indianapolis: Cisco Press, 2011).

[4] Michael Surtees, "Designing and Developing for Mobile Web vs. Native App," Gesture Theory blog, April 27, 2011, http://gesturetheory.com/blog/2011/04/designing-and-developing-for-the-mobile-web-vs-native-app.

[5] The iTunes listing for *Wired Magazine's* iPad app can be found at: http://itunes.apple.com/us/app/wired-magazine/id373903654?mt=8.

[6] Mathew Ingram, Quoted from *Spark* 135, CBC Radio-Canada, January 21, 2011, http://www.cbc.ca/spark/2011/01/spark-135-january-23-26-2011/.

[7] Christopher Butler, "Google Books Wins by Consistent User Interface," www.newfangled.com, March 17, 2011, http://www.newfangled.com/google_books_wins_by_consistent_user_interface.

[8] Joshua Johnson, "20 Amazing Examples of Using Media Queries for Responsive Web Design," Design Shack, May 12, 2011, http://designshack.co.uk/articles/css/20-amazing-examples-of-using-media-queries-for-responsive-web-design.

[9] Ethan Marocotte, *Responsive Web Design* (A Book Apart, 2011).

[10] Dave Mello, "Delivering a Mobile Experience," www.newfangled.com, April 6, 2011, http://www.newfangled.com/mobile_web_development_templates_stylesheets.

9. The Web of Tomorrow

[1] Chris Anderson, "The Web Is Dead, Long Live the Internet," Wired.com, August 17, 2010, http://www.wired.com/magazine/2010/08/ff_webrip/all/1.

[2] In *Time Travel in Einstein's Universe*, physicist J. Richard Gott theorized that we can predict how long something we are presently observing is likely to last. Based upon the Copernican principle—that our present position is inherently ordinary—we can assume that we're currently observing the Web at a random point during its existence, not necessarily any closer to the beginning than the end, nor exactly in the center. Gott's idea is that if there is nothing special about our present position, then there is a 50 percent chance that we're observing the web sometime during the middle two quarters of its overall duration. If we're at the beginning, then one quarter of the web's "lifetime" has already passed, but three quarters are ahead. On the other hand, if we're at the end of the middle portion, then three quarters of its lifetime has already passed and only one quarter remains. That means there is a 50 percent chance that the web has between one-third and three times the years it has already lived left in its future. At the time of this writing, the web has existed for twenty years. Using Gott's theory, we can predict that there is a 50 percent chance that the web has somewhere between 6.66 and 60 years left. Those odds aren't bad, especially for someone like me, whose career relies upon the web.

J. Richard Gott, *Time Travel in Einstein's Universe: The Physical Possibilities of Travel Through Time* (New York: Mariner Books, 2002).

Those not inclined to track this book down and read it are in luck. John Tierney explained the gist of Gott's prediction theory in an article for *the New York Times*.

John Tierney, "A Survival Imperative for Space Colonization," *New York Times*, July 17, 2007, http://www.nytimes.com/2007/07/17/science/17tier.html.

[3] Laika was a Soviet space dog and the first animal to orbit the Earth. A detailed Wikipedia entry telling her story can be found here: http://en.wikipedia.org/wiki/Laika.

[4] J.C.R. Licklider, "Man-Computer Symbiosis," IRE Transactions on Human Factors in Electronics, MIT.edu, March 1960, http://groups.csail.mit.edu/medg/people/psz/Licklider.html.

J.C.R. Licklider, "Memorandum for Members and Affiliates of the Intergalactic Computer Network," Advanced Research Projects Agency, April 23, 1963 (published on the web December 2001), http://www.kurzweilai.net/memorandum-for-members-and-affiliates-of-the-intergalactic-computer-network.

[5] Dr. Lawrence G. Roberts, "The Evolution of Packet Switching," IEEE, Nov 1978 (published on the web in 2001), http://www.packet.cc/files/ev-packet-sw.html.

There are numerous other resources devoted to telling the story of the invention of packet switching. Besides the Wikipedia entry, found here: http://en.wikipedia.org/wiki/Packet_switching, IBiblio.org has a collection of pages devoted to Internet Pioneers, which includes Baran, as well as others mentioned in this chapter (Licklider, Bush and Berners-Lee), located here: http://www.ibiblio.org/pioneers/baran.html. More information about Donald Davies can be found in the biographies collection of The History of Computing Project here: http://www.thocp.net/biographies/davies_donald.htm, as well as Wikipedia, here: http://en.wikipedia.org/wiki/Donald_Davies.

[6] Dr. Lawrence G. Roberts, "Resource Sharing Computer Networks," IEEE, Jun 1968 (published on the web in 2001), http://www.packet.cc/files/res-share-comp-net.html.

[7] John Lienhard, "Vannevar Bush," Engines of Our Ingenuity audio program, University of Houston, http://www.uh.edu/engines/epi1753.htm.

[8] Vannevar Bush, "As We May Think," *The Atlantic*, July 1945, http://www.theatlantic.com/magazine/print/1969/12/as-we-may-think/3881/ (accessed December 23 2010).

[9] I consulted numerous sources on Paul Otlet and Henri La Fontaine. They included:

W. Boyd Rayward, T*he Universe of Information: The Work of Paul Otlet for Documentation and Universal Organization* (Moscow: All-Union Institute for Scientific and Technical Information [VINITI], 1975), http://lib.ugent.be/fulltxt/handle/1854/3989/otlet-universeofinformation.pdf.

W. Boyd Rayward, "The Case of Paul Otlet, Pioneer of Information Science, Internationalist, Visionary: Reflections on Biography," Journal of Librarianship and Information Science (September 23, 1991): 135–145, http://people.lis.illinois.edu/~wrayward/otlet/PAUL_OTLET_REFLECTIONS_ON_BIOG.HTM.

Alle Kennis van de Wereld, *Biography of Paul Otlet* (Noorederlicht, 1998), http://www.archive.org/details/paulotlet/.

And, of course, the Wikipedia entries for Otlet and La Fontaine, respectively, here: http://en.wikipedia.org/wiki/Paul_Otlet#Bibliography and http://en.wikipedia.org/wiki/Henri_La_Fontaine; and the Nobel Prize biography of La Fontaine, found here:

http://nobelprize.org/nobel_prizes/peace/laureates/1913/fontaine-bio.html

[10] This history of course includes the work of Claude Shannon, who is considered to be the father of information theory. A good place to start learning more about information theory would be the Wikipedia entries for information theory and Claude Shannon, found here:

http://en.wikipedia.org/wiki/Information_theory

http://en.wikipedia.org/wiki/Claude_E._Shannon

[11] Stephen Wolfram created a Timeline of Systematic Data and the Development of Computable Knowledge, which blows my simplified timeline out of the water. You can access it here:

http://www.wolframalpha.com/docs/timeline/

[12] Kevin Kelly, *What Technology Wants* (New York: Viking Adult, 2010).

[13] The diversity of opinion on the future of the web is evident in an article for *Technology Review*, which featured the predictions of many well-known tech luminaries:

http://www.technologyreview.com/Infotech/20943/?a=f.

[14] Douglas Ruskoff, "The Next Renaissance," Edge.org, July 10, 2008, http://edge.org/3rd_culture/rushkoff08/rushkoff08_index.html.

[15] GeoCities has been preserved by numerous organizations, most comprehensively, the Internet Archive, which can be accessed here:

http://www.archive.org/web/geocities.php

The most creative preservation of GeoCities was created by Richard Vijgen in 2011, called The Deleted City. Vijgen's presentation can be viewed here: http://deletedcity.net/.

[16] The idea that boredom might influence the future of the web first came to me by way of a quote attributed to Russell Davies, who was reported by James Bridle to have said of the web, people would "probably just get bored with it." You can find that quote here:

James Bridle, "Maps, Books, Spimes, Paper: Post-Digital Media Design at SXSW," BookTwo.org, March 29, 2010, http://booktwo.org/notebook/mbsp-sxsw/.

[17] Kevin Slavin, "Reality Is Plenty, Thanks," dconstruct.org, September 2, 2011, http://2011.dconstruct.org/conference/kevin-slavin.

The video of this presentation can be found here: http://www.youtube.com/watch?v=o03wWtWASW4.

[18] Russell Davies, "Talking on the Radio/The Internet with Things." Russell Davies blog, September 21, 2011, http://russelldavies.typepad.com/planning/2011/09/what-i-meant-to-say-the-internet-with-things.html.

[19] SoundAffects, a project created by students of Parsons the New School for Design, can be found on the Web here:

http://soundaffectsnyc.com/

[20] You can learn more about these innovative firms by visiting their websites:

http://www.stamen.com/

http://www.rockwellgroup.com

http://www.berglondon.com/

http://www.dentsulondon.com/

ACKNOWLEDGMENTS

Thank you to Patrick Demasco, my stepfather, for introducing me to technology. In the early 1980s, he brought home the first computer I had ever seen. He helped me learn my first programming language (Visual BASIC in the second grade), showed me robots in his research lab and gave me my first UI design job—not to mention his entire catalog of *Wired* magazines, which continue to inspire me today. Far more milestones like these make up a rich background in technology and design that was sparked and nurtured largely by him. I must also thank the rest of my family for their role in making me who I am. I'm deeply fortunate to have a very large family that loves me, but unfortunate that they are too many to adequately thank here. You know who you are!

I'm grateful to also be a part of the Newfangled family, which has enabled me to learn a great deal, be involved in exciting work and meet many wonderful people over the past eight years, and of course, for Eric Holter, who created Newfangled and, in doing so, opened doors for me that I'm so very fortunate to have passed through. I also owe very special thanks to Mark O'Brien for his presence in my life: for trusting me, believing in me, challenging me and being a pleasure to know.

Thank you to the entire F+W Media team: Gary Lynch, for suggesting I write this; Megan Patrick, for helping shape the project in its early stages; Suzanne Lucas for guiding me through the fine print; Amy Owen and Lauren Mosko Bailey, my editors, for all of their work; and Grace Ring for turning the manuscript into a real-life object. Thanks, also, to my editors at *Print* magazine: Aaron Kenedi, Michael Silverberg, Judy Grover and James Gaddy, for offering me opportunities to explore many of the ideas contained in this book in their magazine and online.

Many others—Justin Kerr, Michael Babwahsingh, David Baker, Vitaly Friedman, Silas Munro, Sarah Dooley, Keith McCoy, Lindsey Barlow, Martin Demasco, David Sherwin, Ray Delaney and Rafael Kushick— offered invaluable insights, opinions and assistance as I wrote this book. Thank you all.

ABOUT THE
AUTHOR

Christopher Butler is Chief Operating Officer of Newfangled, a web development firm on the cutting edge of modern digital marketing and technology, where he spends most of his time sharing what he has learned about the web with his colleagues and clients, as well as managing the personnel and systems that keep Newfangled producing.

A graduate of the Rhode Island School of Design, Christopher has remained an active design educator and enthusiast. He has returned to RISD as both a visiting critic and adjunct faculty and has served as a juror for the REBRAND 100 Awards. He is also a member of the HOW Interactive Design Conference advisory board.

In addition to writing regularly at Newfangled.com, Christopher's writing has also appeared in *Smashing Magazine, Print* magazine and *HOW*. You can also find him blogging periodically at http://chrbutler.com and tweeting incessantly @chrbutler.

INDEX

MORE GREAT TITLES FROM HOW BOOKS

The Web Designer's Idea Book Series

By Patrick McNeil

This must-have series features the best of the best website examples from the popular blog, DesignMeltdown.com that are sure to inspire as well as educate on new trends and improvements. These books are arranged thematically, so no matter what kind of website you're tackling you'll be able to easily browse through top examples of successful design.

The Designer's Web Handbook

By Patrick McNeil

Web guru Patrick McNeil teaches you the fundamentals of great web design. He explains how to make a website not only look good, but work as well. Too many designers are unaware of the differences they'll face when designing for the web. This book will help you avoid making those costly mistakes so that your designs work the way you want them to.

Above the Fold

By Brian D. Miller

This is a different kind of web design book. Above the Fold is not about timely design or technology trends; instead, this book is about the timeless fundamentals of effective communication within the context of web design. It tackles the considerations that web designers must make when developing successful web sites.

Find these books and many others at MyDesignShop.com or your local bookstore.

Special Offer From HOW Books!

You can get 15% off your entire order at MyDesignShop.com! All you have to do is go to www.howdesign.com/howbooks-offer and sign up for our free e-newsletter on graphic design. You'll also get a free digital download of HOW magazine.

 For more news, tips and articles, follow us at Twitter.com/HOWbrand

 For behind-the-scenes information and special offers, become a fan at Facebook.com/HOWmagazine

 For visual inspiration, follow us at Pinterest.com/HOWbrand